D0870130

Grief:
The Great Yearning

By

Pat Bertram

Clear Light Books
Published by Indigo Sea Press
Winston-Salem

Clear Light Books
Indigo Sea Press
302 Ricks Drive
Winston-Salem, NC 27103

This is the true story of one woman's emotions and experiences as she journeyed through grief. It is not intended to reflect everyone's experience with grief, nor is it intended to be a substitute for professional help.

First Clear Light Books edition published
April, 2016
Clear Light Books, Moon Sailor, and all production design are trademarks of Indigo Sea Press, used under license.

For information regarding bulk purchases of this book, digital purchase and special discounts, please contact the publisher at indigoseapress.com

Cover design by Pat Bertram (photo by D. Bertram)

Manufactured in the United States of America

ISBN 978-1-63066-369-8

For Jeff,

without whom this book would never
have been written

Introduction

Death came in the spring.

At the beginning of March, the doctors said that Jeff, my life mate—my soul mate—had inoperable kidney cancer and that he had six months to live. He had only three weeks. We'd spent thirty-four years together, and suddenly I was alone, unprepared, and totally devastated. I couldn't even begin to comprehend the wreckage of my life. It wasn't just he who died but "we." There was no more "us," no more shared plans and dreams and private jokes. There was only me.

Other losses compounded the misery. I had to sort through the accumulation of decades, dismantle what was left of our life, move from our home. We bereft are counseled not to make major changes during the first year after a significant loss—one's thinking processes become muddled, leaving one prey to faulty logic and rash decisions—but I needed to go stay with my father for a while. Although he was doing well by himself, he was 93 years old, and it wasn't wise for him to continue living alone.

I relocated from cool mountain climes to the heat of a southwestern community. Lost, heartbroken, awash in tears, I walked for hours every day beneath the cloudless sky, finding what comfort I could in the simple activity. During one such walk, I turned down an unfamiliar city street, and followed it . . . into the desert.

I was stunned to find myself in a vast wilderness of rocky knolls, creosote bushes, cacti, rabbits, lizards, and snakes. I'd been to the area several times during my mother's last few months, but I'd spent little time outside. I hated the heat, the constant glare of the sun, the harsh winds. After Jeff died, however, that bleak weather, that bleak terrain seemed to mirror my inner landscape. Wandering in the desert, crying in the wilderness, I tried to find meaning in all that had happened. I didn't find it, of course. How can there be meaning in the painful, horrific death of a 63-year-old man? I didn't find myself, either. It was too soon for me to move on, to abandon my grief. I felt as if I'd be negating him and the life we led.

What I did find was the peace of the moment.

Children, most of whom know little of death and the horrors of life, live in the moment because they can—it's all they have. The bereft, who know too much about death and the horrors of life, live in the moment because they must—it's the only way they can survive.

During the first year after Jeff's death, I lived as a child—moment to moment, embracing my grief, trying not to think about the future because such thoughts brought panic about growing old alone, trying not to think about the past because such thoughts reminded me of all I had lost.

And so went the seasons of my soul. The spring of death gave way to the summer of grief, and grief flowed into the fall and winter of renewal.

This book is not a how-to but a how-done, a compilation of letters, blog posts, and journal entries I wrote while struggling to survive my first year of grief. As you journey through grief, I hope you will find comfort in knowing you are not alone. Whatever you feel, others have felt. Whatever seemingly crazy thing you do to bring yourself comfort, others have done. And, as impossible as it is to imagine now, you will survive.

First Month

Day 1, **Grief Journal,**
At 1:40 this morning, Jeff died as courageously as he lived.

Seven weeks ago, he was overcome with debilitating pain. We'd been through such crises so many times before, I thought he'd plummeted to another low plateau where he would remain for months if not years. Not that I wanted him to be in agony—perhaps I thought the pain would go away? But he knew it was the end, knew what he'd have to face. To gather his courage, he told me stories of his bravery—how as a young runner he could not give up even when injured. He told me about all the times he hurt his ankles, his knees, and still he never gave up.

We were so close that day. During the last year of his long illness, I'd forgotten why I loved him. We'd driven each other nuts—he trying to prepare me for the end, me gritting my teeth and clenching my fists in irritation because I did not want to hear of his dying. (Through it all, though, we always gravitated toward each other, always cared for each other.). But that day I remembered why I loved him. And I fell in love all over again.

He never did give up. Despite pain, drugs, and massive tumors in his body and brain, he tried to live and to accomplish something. It was heartbreaking to watch. In the end, his body gave out—there was nothing left but bones and skin. And the tumors that ate him alive.

I feel doubly cheated—not just out of sharing the coming years with him, but of not even being able to share a few months of renewed closeness.

And now *I* have to be brave.

I do not know how I am going to survive. I don't know why I was so naïve, but I truly didn't think his death would devastate me. I've lived with his dying for so long, I thought I'd gone through all the stages of grief. Turns out, I went

3

through all the stages except grief itself. The immensity of the pain is way too much for me to handle. I told him—and it's the truth (I think)—that I'll be okay in the long run. It's the short run that will kill me if I don't find a way to get a grip on myself. I miss him more than I ever imagined. My chest hurts and I feel sick to my stomach. I am in too much agony to cry when I am by myself, though I cannot talk to anyone without tears streaming down my face.

I'm honored that he shared his life with me. I'm glad I got to be there at the end, though I wish, with all my being, he didn't have to go.

Day 2, **Dear Jeff,**

I was out walking today, trying to figure out how to get through the rest of my life without you, when it dawned on me—I can write you. I can still tell you everything I'm doing and thinking, still ask your advice, still use you as a sounding board to think things through. It might help me feel close to you, feel as if you're still part of my life.

I never thought I'd watch television and your video tapes again—it was something I did only with you. I didn't feel comfortable watching on my own, probably because I grew up without television. But tonight I rewound the last *Boston Legal* tape you made and watched for a couple of hours. It felt sad but good. I imagined you sitting next to me, and I relaxed enough to fall asleep through a show or two. Sleeping sort of defeats the point of watching, but mostly I liked to watch tapes with you so we could be together. In that regard, the tape served its purpose.

Afterward, I gathered your drugs and medical paraphernalia and set them on the kitchen counter. The hospice people are supposed to come and dispose of them tomorrow. I'm going to work backwards—get everything back the way it was before you signed up for hospice, then start going through your things. Should I keep all your tapes, even the ones I will never watch? Right now, I am incapable of making decisions of any kind. It's only been forty-four hours since you died, but it feels as though I've been crying for years. And screaming. I was wandering around the living room, clutching my middle, holding back the howls of distress, when I realized no one would hear if I screamed, and so I did.

I miss you, and I suspect that I always will. I love you.

Day 3, **Grief Journal**

This was a hard day, though I don't suppose any of them will be easy for a while. It's amazing how little energy I have. I can't do much at all. Today I rewound some of Jeff's video tapes, the ones we watched toward the end. Perhaps tomorrow I will find the strength to put them away.

The hospice nurse came and got rid of the drugs. (Dumped them in a plastic bag of kitty litter, which turned them into a solidified mess, and took them with her.) The medical supply people are supposed to come tomorrow to pick up the oxygen tank. It's like I'm rewinding his life. I wish I could rewind it back to the good times. We did have good times. I know we did. But everything got so muddled at the end. All we were doing was struggling to survive.

I can't believe there was ever a time I wished the struggle were over so I could start my new life. How could I not have known I'd feel such pain? I heard today that losing a long-time mate was like an amputation, and that's exactly what this feels like.

Good, bad, indifferent—it was all the same. We were together. We took care of each other. And now he's been amputated from me and my life.

I got furious on his account today. It's so unfair that he had such ill health, that his life ended too soon and too terribly. It seems unreal, now, that we took for granted he would die young. Shouldn't we have railed against it more? But he was so disciplined, focusing his energies on trying to prolong his life and be productive.

I don't know which is worse, the times I miss him dreadfully or the times I concentrate on doing something and he drifts from my thoughts. It seems such a betrayal. If he only exists in my memory and I don't think about him, it's as if he's dying again. And once was hard enough. It takes my breath away when I realize I will never talk to him again. Well, I will talk to him, and I do, but we will never converse. I will never hear his voice.

I thought I was through telling people our sad little tale, but I've remembered a few others I have to notify about his being dead. I hope I don't start crying when I talk to them. I'm tired of crying, tired of feeling sick to my stomach, tired of the hole in my chest. How do people endure such grief for months on end? I truly hate that he's gone. Hate it!!

Day 4, **Dear Jeff,**
Another rough day. They came and picked up the oxygen tank. I am glad to see it leave. I chopped up the tubing from your nasal cannula. How you hated that thing and wanted to cut it off! So I cut it up for you. You'll never have to use it again.

I opened a new bank account though I'm going to keep our joint account. I know you won't need money, but I'll keep some in the account in case you do. I talked to the woman at the bank for a long time. She's going through a divorce after being married for twenty-five years. There are many similarities in our grief, but there is one huge difference—you are gone from this world, and her husband is not. I could deal with your absence a lot easier if I knew you were well and happy.

I'm trying to think of something new to tell you, but it's all the same. Just missing you, feeling sick to my stomach, having trouble eating and breathing because of the pain of amputation, spending way too much time crying. The hole you left in my life will always be there. I love you.

Day 5, **Dear Jeff,**
I cried at odd moments today. Well, I cried after I got angry with you for being gone. Textbook. Strange, isn't it, to be following those typical patterns? I cleared out a lot of food and took it to the senior center. I don't know if you would have liked that, but I kept thinking that if you didn't

want me to donate your food, you shouldn't have died. Silly, huh?

I've been reflecting on the past year when you became someone I didn't know. I bet it was the metastases in your brain (and the pain) that turned you into a stranger. I don't know what would have been harder—to reconnect the way we did and lose you twice or not reconnect and have to live with extra regrets.

Regrets—boy, do I have them. I regret I didn't have one more day with you, that I let the nurse talk me into taking you to the hospice care center to live out your last few days. I regret I took your dying for granted. I regret I didn't spend more time with you that last year. I know you coped better on your own, and you wanted to be left alone, but I feel as if I let you down. I continued my own life while you were dying—in fact, you encouraged me to do new things—but the end came so quickly. I feel as if your whole life—our life together, anyway—flashed before my eyes and winked out. I cannot comprehend the meaning of your life, though perhaps it's not my place to make sense of it.

I love you. I wish I had told you that more often.

Day 5, Blog Post, **A Tribute to a Fallen Mate**

Once upon a time I wrote snippets of poetry. That time coincided to when I met the man who would share my life, and some of the snippets I wrote are poignant to me now because they chronicle my first feelings for him. A private man, he would be appalled that I am writing about him, but I didn't want his life to pass unnoticed by all but me. Though written long ago, this bit still fits him:

> you give
> (not lightly
> the figments of this world
> but)
> your reality
> and your radiance
> (your soul)

Day 6, **Dear Jeff,**

I started crying today and couldn't stop. I had to go to town to break up the crying jag, otherwise I might have cried all day. I'm glad you'll never have to go through this. I cling to that thought—that your death spared you ever having to grieve for me. We did so much together, and now our paths have divided. I can't yet follow you. Are you gone? Snuffed out forever? Or does something of you remain somewhere? Are you warm? Fed? Have plenty of cold liquids to drink? Thinking about what happened to you makes me sick to my stomach still. The days after your diagnosis went by too fast. I still can't comprehend your suffering or your dying.

I sometimes hear noises out in the living room when I am in the bedroom, and my first thought is that it's you. It comes as a shock when I realize . . . again . . . that you're dead. I truly don't know how to get along without you. Or, more accurately, I don't want to get along without you. You were my life for so many years. I wonder what my future holds. Love? Success? Failure? Loneliness?

I still can't decide if I want to get rid of almost everything we own or put it in storage. I know I'll hate having re-minders of everything I've lost, but perhaps there will come a time when our things bring me comfort?

I don't know what to do about your car. Keep it? Sell it? Donate it?

I don't suppose you want to hear about these indecisions, but they do loom in my thoughts. I talk to you all day, but when it comes time to write you, I can only think of such trivialities. Yet that's what our life together ended up being. I wanted only the cosmically important things to be part of our shared life, yet it devolved into basic survival, errands, household chores. I'm keeping up with the chores. Sort of.

When I was at the grocery store, the clerk asked where you were, so I told her. She hugged me and cried with me. Not enough tears have been shed for you—no amount of tears will ever be enough—so those tears gave me comfort. Your life—and death—shouldn't pass lightly.

Day 7, **Dear Jeff,**

Today was very long. I can't even remember what I did this morning. I know I didn't talk to a single person all day. How pathetic is that? I suppose I could have called someone, but what could I have said? I only want to talk about you, and that makes me cry.

I can't believe how terrible I feel. I know I keep saying I didn't expect this, but it's the truth. I also think I lied to you when I said I would be okay. Right now, I'd just as soon die and be done with it. There's a chance that eventually I will be okay, as I told you, but getting there is going to be rougher than I could ever have imagined. Did you hear me scream for you today? You didn't answer, so I'm assuming you couldn't, for whatever reason.

I'm getting over the worst of the horror I felt at the way you died, so now I'm mourning the whole of your life. I miss you more than I ever thought possible. You were my soul mate. Good and bad, we were together for so long that you leave a big hole. I don't think it will ever be filled. I don't think it can be.

I hate that you're gone. I wish you were here so I could tell you how much I love you.

Day 7, Blog Post, **Searching For Happy Memories**

I've been searching for happy memories to take the edge off the memory of watching my life mate die so painfully, and one I've been thinking about a lot lately is a day I visited him at To Your Health, the store he owned. (That's how we met; I was a customer at his health food store.) That particular day, we spent hours talking—about life, books, history, moving from one topic to another as easily as if we'd known each other a lifetime instead of just a few months—and then he walked me outside. This is the poem I wrote when I got home that night:

> you turned around
> and waved to me
> after we said good-bye

a small gesture
that told me more
than all the words
we had spoken

I wish I could have just one more word from him, one more wave, one more minute with him at his store.

Day 8, **Dear Jeff,**

I picked up your ashes today. (And your blue pillowcase. The woman from the funeral home was late, so I went to the hospice care center to pick up the pillowcase the caregivers had misplaced. I don't know why I was so insistent on getting it back, but I kept after them until they found it. Perhaps I felt scattered? Needed to put everything right?)

Your ashes are heavy! Of course, they're not ashes but minerals, inorganic matter, pulverized bone, the part of you that was never alive—but that's all I have left of you. I hope you're not upset, but I'm not going to scatter them, at least not yet. A minister friend suggested I keep some of them.

Since I don't know what else to do with them (except dump them in the Gunnison River and hope they wend safe to sea) I decided to follow his advice. Oddly, the thought of keeping your ashes brings me comfort. And I'm keeping all of them. I can't bear to parcel out what is left of you. So your "cremains," as they so cutely call them in the funeral business, are still in your temporary "urn," which is nothing but a box made out of some sort of plastic.

Typically, the brass urn I ordered has been discontinued, so they're ordering another and will ship it to me. I wrapped your robe around your temporary urn. I keep remembering how cold you were at the end. It also makes the urn huggable. Don't laugh, but I hugged your ashes and thought about the last time we embraced. We held each other a long time that morning, knowing we'd never hug again.

I assumed that as time went on I would grieve less, but that is not the case. The more you recede from me, the more I see the whole of our lives, and the more I see, the more I find to grieve. It's not just you who are dead but "us." There is no "us" anymore. I can't fathom that. Part of me doesn't believe you're dead. I still feel sick to my stomach at the thought. I wish you were here. Wish we could talk. Wish I could hug you for real.

Day 11, **Dear Jeff,**

I cried on and off all day. If you were here, I'd hide in my office so you couldn't see my tears and feel bad for me, but then, if you were here, I wouldn't be grieving. I'm not sure I ever understood our connection. No matter what happened to us or between us, there was always that caring concern for each other that went deeper than any emotion.

I thought I was doing okay—didn't cry much yesterday, but today . . .

When you were dying and the people at hospice would express their concern for my welfare, I'd tell them they needed to concentrate on you, that I had the rest of my life to deal with my grief. Well, now it's time for me, but I'd rather not have to deal with this anguish. I'd rather deal with you, a strong, healthy, happy *living* you, but no one is asking what I prefer. So, here I am, and there you are.

I wish I could take off for a couple of weeks. Don't know where I'd go, but I'd like to run away from myself and my grief. I wish I could run to the past when we still had dreams and expectations. I feel as if there is much unfinished business from our life together, but you're not here to help finish it. And yet, at the end, we were able to say everything we needed to say to each other. Not everyone gets that opportunity.

I miss you. I love you. I can't bear your being gone.

Day 12, **Dear Jeff,**

I am having a hard time dealing with your death. I have moments when I can pretend I'm doing okay, but then I fall apart, sometimes for no reason. I know losing someone—a mate—is not uncommon, but I have not lost you before. I hate using that word "lose" as if I've just misplaced you. I know one does not die from this pain—at least not always— but it sure feels as if it could kill me.

I truly am glad you don't have to suffer any more, but I don't see why you had to suffer at all. When I told the hospice social worker that it wasn't fair, that you hadn't had much of a life, she said, "As difficult as it is to understand, he did have a life—being sick was his life." *What?* Makes no sense to me, but none of this does.

I've been watching *Boston Legal*—it makes me feel close to you since it was one of the last things you taped and it was the last thing we watched together. I have your robe-wrapped ashes on the couch with me. If I catch a glimpse of your robe out of the corner of my eye, I can almost convince myself that you're really with me. I should probably get rid of that emotional crutch, put your ashes someplace where I would not have to see them all the time, but I like having you on the couch with me.

I've cried so much recently—real crying, tears and sobs, not just a few silent tears—that it's beginning to seem phony. As if I'm forcing it. But maybe I need the wailing to balance out the pain, to help ease it. I know I keep saying it, but it's the truth—I hate that you're gone. I pound your punching bag when I get angry, as I often do. Tears, then rage. How horribly classic.

Day 15, **Grief Journal**

It's been two weeks since Jeff died. Feels like he's been gone forever, but my emotions are still as raw as if he left this very moment. I hug his ashes at least once every day. I go into paroxysms of sobbing and crying a couple of times a day. I worry way too much about what to do with our stuff.

Although I'd made the decision to go stay with my father, I still vacillate, wondering if I should remain here. This is where Jeff and I lived for more than two decades. I feel as if by going, I'm leaving him to fend for himself. The conventional wisdom is not to make any major changes for a year, and yet, what is here for me without him? It's not as if I'm leaving my home—my home already left me. Whatever our lives were, whatever Jeff meant to me, he was my home.

There is no trauma in the past thirty-four years I had to face alone. Now I am going through the biggest trauma of my life—dealing with his absence—and I have to do it by myself. I'm not sure I have the courage to start over, to live without his companionship. He knew me so well. He knew my ideas, my values, my hopes. I never had to explain my beliefs—he lived them with me.

I wish he were here to comfort me, to tell me I'll be fine, to help me decide what to do. I wish he were here to hug me one more time. To watch one more movie with me. To say one more word.

Day 16, Blog Post, **What to Say to Someone Who is Grieving**

After I notified people of my mate's death, few sent an acknowledgement. When I mentioned this to a friend, she said perhaps it was because they did not know what to say. This is probably true. Most comments posted to me on various discussion threads began with: "I don't know what to say." Of course, being writers, these people followed that statement with very touching responses, but I also received touching remarks from non-writers. To be honest, all responses mean a lot to me—grief is such an isolating experience, that any indication of concern helps remind me that people do care, that perhaps I'm not totally alone after all.

If you cannot think of anything eloquent to say in the face of another's grief, say something simple. Say, "I'm sorry." Say, "I'm thinking about you." Say, "My heart goes out to you." Say, "I shed tears for you." And there is always the standard, "My thoughts and prayers are with you."

If you knew the deceased, talk about him. The bereaved (a terrible word, so namby-pamby and doesn't really connote how truly bereft one is after such a loss) will find comfort in your memories. If you didn't know him, you can talk about your own experiences with the death of a loved one, though be aware that grief piled upon grief might be a bit overwhelming for the one left behind. Despite that, the stories people share with me make me realize that though the pain seems impossible to live through, it will eventually become tolerable. At least, I hope it will.

Many people told me to "hang in there," but although well meaning, it is not, perhaps, the best thing to say to someone who is grieving. Depression is a part of the process, and "hanging in there" makes one wonder "hanging from what? And where?" (If you are one of those who used this expression, I hope I'm not hurting your feelings. Rest assured I took your words in the spirit offered, and was pleased that you thought of me.)

If you truly cannot find words of your own, share a poem that helped you get through your grief. Although grief is such a personal experience, the emotions portrayed in poetry are universal.

If you can't think of something to say immediately, but eventually think of the perfect thing, say it then. It is never too late. Grief lasts a very long time. As the days, weeks, months pass, others forget, but the person who is grieving doesn't. Any indication that you are thinking of her in her sorrow is comforting.

In the end, it doesn't really matter what you say. Extending a bit of comfort, showing that you haven't forgotten, showing that you care—those are the important things.

Day 17, Blog Post, **Baby Steps**

I've heard that the death of a mate and the ensuing grief change a person, and perhaps this is true. If one is part of a couple, when he dies, so does the "we." One cannot be the same after such a splitting apart. The world one lives in cannot be the same.

I feel like a toddler, taking shaky steps in this newly alien and dangerous world. I exercised this morning, took my vitamins with a protein drink, wrote a letter to my deceased mate (the only writing besides blogging I am doing at the moment), and I took a walk. I even managed to eat. The one thing I had never expected was how the thought of his being gone makes me sick to my stomach. When I do eat, I eat healthy, though. I got rid of all snacks a while back, so what's in the house is real food.

All these baby steps that I'm taking serve to take me further away from him, deeper into . . . I don't know what. I just wish I could skip the coming months of pain and go directly to the part where I emerge strong, wise, confident, and capable of handling anything. But, ironically, the coming months of pain will be the catalyst to making me what I will become.

Day 18, **Dear Jeff,**

I'm going to keep the punching bag I made you. When anger overwhelms me, it helps to punch the dang thing.

I am so very sorry that you are gone. I cannot bear to think of what you suffered. I cannot bear to think of you worrying about me while you were dying. I cannot bear to think of living without you. I cannot bear to think of anything, and yet I wonder. Is there a purpose to all this? A purpose to my life? A purpose to yours? Is there some sort of higher power? Some sort of consciousness after death? Will we meet again, or is death truly the end? Was it fate that we met? Fate that you died? It makes no sense to me that we were brought together and then ripped apart.

I have moments of panic when I realize you are gone from this earth. It's as if the ground has been pulled out from beneath me, and I am dangling in open space with nothing beneath my feet. I panic when I realize we will never talk to each other. We'll never fix meals together. We will never laugh together or get irritated at each other. You will never smile at me. We will never hug. (I still hug your ashes every day. I need that connection, however phony it might be.)

I am sorry for my selfishness that last year. I was unable to cope with the thought of your dying, so I blocked it out. Mostly, I'd decided that even if you were dying, I had to live. And so I did. Or at least tried to. Odd how none of that struggling to live has made this time any easier. I thought I'd moved on. Turns out I was wrong.

I just realized I envy you. You are out of it. I'm the one who has to go on, though I'd just as soon be out of it, too. I don't want to go through all the horror you did, so I will take care of myself as best as I can to delay my end as long as possible. But still, if I had the option of not waking up, would I take it? I don't know. I would like to be done with the pain of living, but I'd also like to see what, if anything, I become. You took me as far as you could on my journey through life. The rest I'll have to do on my own.

I miss you, and I know I'll eventually have to let you go, but all of this is too raw still. I'm tired of crying, but I'm afraid if I try to stop myself, I'll prolong the grieving process. I'll always grieve for you, but this process is about to kill me. Or maybe make me stronger, considering how much I punch the bag.

Day 19, Grief Journal

I've been worried about my behavior toward Jeff the last year of his life. It's not that I treated him badly—I didn't, not really—but as he drew away from me further into the world of dying, I got more adamant about living my own life. Very callous, but perhaps the best thing for me. Or not. If I had grieved that last year, would I be grieving so much now?

It's been said that every behavior is a matter of survival, which I suppose is true in my case. I could feel myself fighting to live, to gain more autonomy, but that struggle manifested itself in impatience, irritability, and resentment. I think I was angry at his condition and took it out on him. When I remember all the years I swallowed my feelings in deference to his illness, it appalls me that at the end, I couldn't sustain it. I am so not the person I thought I was!

The brain has a way of blocking out what it can't handle. If I had truly known what was going on with Jeff, I would have been more patient with him, but it would have killed me. No, it wouldn't have killed me, but it would have felt like it. I find myself wishing I had his last year to live over, but then I get horrified at myself. If I lived that year over again to assuage my sense of self, I'd be condemning him to live over a year of hell. I'll have to learn to accept my behavior and forgive it. Jeff did. He understood.

Even though he often talked that last year about wanting it to be finished, when it came to the end, he didn't want to go. I will always remember that last day he spent at home. We had just made the decision that he would go to the hospice care center for a few days to give me a chance to sleep. (His terminal restlessness kept us both up all night, and neither of us was getting any sleep. Although it was supposed to be a five-day respite, we knew he was never coming back.) He was sitting on the couch, so small, momentarily comfortable. He gave me a pitiful smile and said, with a crack in his voice, "I don't want to go. We have a good life here. We're doing okay, aren't we? I'm not ready for you to throw me away." About broke my heart.

I wish I could have kept him home one more day, but I got scared. He hated the nasal cannula, and I found him frantically rummaging in a kitchen drawer for a knife to cut it off. What if . . . ? No, I'm not even going to think about that.

I still don't understand how anyone survives the loss of a long-time mate. It truly is an amputation. Forever after, he will be absent. Every single minute of the rest of my life, he will not be here. How is it possible to survive such pain?

Day 20, **Grief Journal**

I wonder if I'll ever feel completely happy again. Jeff's death has left such a hole in my life that I cannot imagine ever being happy except, perhaps, for short periods. I've never been particularly happy—well, that's not true. I was very happy being with him for many years—but I am of a melancholy bent. Is this my nature or only the way things worked out? I can see me struggling to be happy, to grasp every possible bit of felicity in the future. It's the only way to make one's end worthwhile. Dying is such a terrible thing.

I've been angry and resentful that the three to six months of life the doctors predicted after Jeff's diagnosis did not materialize, but considering everything—how weak he was, how the drugs affected him, how restless he was—it's good he didn't have to hang on those extra months.

Life never treated him very well. I tried to be good to him, and I think I succeeded most of the time, but this last year or so I just could not handle the situation any more. He was still here but not. Still him but not.

I don't know how I will feel about going places (both intangible places and geographical places) where he cannot follow, yet it's in those places that I will find a measure of peace.

I'm trying be at peace with Jeff's death. Except for the very end, he was ready to go. At least, he said he was ready. I've been thinking that I could have kept him home longer if I'd drugged him more heavily, but how could I have taken away what remained of his lucidity? I try to hold on to the memory of those last sweet moments—walking hand-in-hand around the living room, his final kiss, his endearments.

How strange that we never used endearments until the very end. A few nights before he died, he said, "Adios, compadre," in a jaunty voice after I got him ready for bed.

The next night he said, "Goodnight, sweetie pie." The last night we were together, he kissed me and said, "I love you, sweetheart."

In an odd sort of way, these moments, precious as they are, are every bit as painful as the rest of his dying because they were not him. Or maybe they were a hint of what our life could have been if he hadn't suffered for all those years? Still, I miss the playful him at the end. I miss the loving him at the beginning. I miss him, the him I had for all the years in between. The thought of his being gone makes me so very queasy. So sad. So angry.

Day 21, **Grief Journal**

Life treated Jeff so dreadfully, it's hard to put a good slant on his fate. He almost died eighteen years ago, and he was seldom healthy after that, though the doctors never figured out what was wrong until it was way too late. (Admittedly, Jeff gave up on doctors for a while. And I'm glad he did. I've been hearing such horror stories lately of the way people died under a doctor's care, with all the "heroic" efforts the doctor made to keep them alive, that in comparison, Jeff's end was peaceful.)

I used to be afraid that he would linger, getting sicker and sicker, until I was too old to start over. (Which, considering how I feel now would not have been such a terrible thing. Looking ahead at all the bleak years to come, I'd just as soon be at the end of life instead of, perhaps, starting the final third. So many potential years to live without him!) At times I felt his long illness was suffocating me with no way out. His death freed us both. I'm trying not to look at the "what ifs"—what our lives would have been like if he'd been healthy—and just look at the "was's." He was sick and in horrible pain. His body was failing him. His brain was failing him.

I'm glad I was able to be there for him during his final weeks. It scares me to think of having to go through that alone when my time comes—it terrifies me, actually—so it brings me a bit of comfort to think that maybe my presence brought him a bit of comfort.

I'm glad he'll never have to watch me die, glad he'll never have to dispose of my "effects," glad he will never have to grieve for me. He would have handled it as bravely as he did everything else, but I'm thankful I can give this gift to him—the gift of my grief (though he would hate to be the cause of so much pain).

I don't know what his life meant, I only know what it meant to me. He set me on the road to becoming a woman, helped me grow up, at least to the extent that I am grown up, helped me become a writer. He was a big part of my life, but I'm not sure I ever knew who he was deep down in his soul. I don't think he ever wanted me to know. I know there were painful times in his past he never told me about, dreams he had, thoughts. But the part I knew, I loved. I don't think he ever knew how much I loved him. And now he never will.

Day 22, Blog Post, **Grief Update**

It's been three weeks since my life mate died. I feel as if I am in an emotional whirlpool, spinning round and round, never quite knowing where I am or where I am going. I have days of relative calm where I can be glad he is finally at peace, then something happens to remind me of my loss, and grief pulls me under. Most recently, I was cleaning photos out of my computer when I came across an image of him I didn't know I had. (We did not take pictures of each other, so the only other photo I have was taken 15 years ago, and it does not look like him at all, though it did at the time.) Last August, we took a trip to the north rim of the Black Canyon. (It's only 20 miles away, but because of the bad road, it might as well have been 200.) The photo I found is of him, alone in that desolate place, with his back to me, looking at . . . eternity, perhaps.

I never expected to grieve deeply. He was sick for so long and in such pain that we didn't have much of a life together the past year or two. I struggled to live while he was dying and thought I succeeded, but nothing prepared me for this total devastation. It turns out that all of it, the good and bad, was part of our life together. In the movie *Three to Tango* is a film clip of a movie I have never seen—I think it's *Of Human Bondage*. The woman in the clip asks: "Will we be happy?" He answers, "No, but does it matter?" And, for us, it didn't matter, at least where each other was concerned. We were connected, no matter what. And now that connection is broken. And I feel that I am broken, too.

I know someday I will find my way again. I know someday I will be able to laugh, to find joy in living again. I know that someday I might even find joy in new love. But for now, I don't know how to be.

Day 23, **Grief Journal**

I was lonely last year with Jeff spending so much time in bed, but now I am so lonely I feel bleak. And bereft. There seems to be little reason to live. No, I am not suicidal, but if I were to die today, I would not care.

I feel as if I am disappearing, fading from life, and all that is left is pain. How anyone gets through this, I do not know. And for what? Life didn't seem foolish when Jeff was alive. I always knew we were meant for each other, but I never realized that he was my tie to life, to wanting to live. Finding that desire in myself right now is next to impossible. All I see are tenuous hopes and promises of pain. It's not enough. Not nearly enough.

Do I need someone in order for my life to have meaning? Sounds weak. But isn't love a major component of life? I know people survive quite nicely on their own, managing to find purpose, but I am so lost. So unhappy.

Perhaps the future holds something good for me, but that is such a silly word to pin my life on, yet that's all I have—"perhaps". Jeff no longer even has that. I'm trying to find comfort in knowing he is no longer suffering, and for a moment yesterday I even envied him. I wish my pain were over, too.

I've developed a terrible fear of dying. I could not handle dying the way Jeff did. It took him so long—years of getting sicker and weaker. Years of pain. I'm truly glad he isn't suffering any more; I just wish he never had to suffer at all. Wish he were here, happy and healthy.

So many foolish wishes. Nothing I can say or do will change anything. The past is done. Finished. It scares me that I have no clear image of him in my mind, but my mind has never been a pictorial one—it's more about feelings and impressions.

I miss him. Miss his fleeting sweet smiles. He had so little to smile about, yet he did smile at me. Did I return his smiles? I hope so. I loved him. Even when I could barely tolerate him (and there were such moments), I still loved him.

I've been worried about how I treated him this past year, yet all things considered, we both dealt quite well with the horrendously emotional and painful time. Not perfectly, but pretty darn good.

Day 23, **Grief Journal**

I've had a jaw infection for weeks, and it won't heal. I went to the dentist and got another course of penicillin. I hope it helps. Grieving is a big part of why I'm not healing since grief depresses the immune system.

I tried not to cry on Thursday and mostly succeeded, then

I totally lost it on Friday and Saturday. (I always cry now on Friday and Saturday. He died late Friday night or early Saturday morning depending on how you look at it, and my body seems to look at it both ways.) I'm fairly calm now, but exhausted.

I wish I could go to sleep for a couple of weeks, or better yet, forever. I am tired of all this emotion, tired of this jaw infection, tired of all these tears, tired of trying to figure out how to get rid of our excess stuff, tired of trying to figure out how to move, tired of living without Jeff, tired of trying to find a reason to live. Mostly, I'm tired of being tired.

I wish I could lose myself in writing, but I'm too tired to think. I wish I were the kind of author who can sit down, put pencil to paper, and let the words flow. I can do this now, here in these pages, but this is stream of consciousness writing, not made-up, though I wish it were. I wish it were a fictional character feeling so lost and agonized and bereft.

It seems a betrayal to go on with my life, but what other choice is there? I am afraid, though. Afraid of growing old alone. Of being old alone. Of dying alone. Of living alone. No wonder grief is so hard—it encompasses a thousand different emotions, none of them good.

Day 24, Blog Post, **The Problem With Grief**

The problem with grief is its immensity. If it were only a matter of being sad that the loved one is gone, as I thought grief was, it would still be hard but doable. Instead, grief affects every part of your life. It's not just a matter of the person being dead, but also all hopes, dreams, plans, expectations that you had with him. If there were a misunderstanding of any kind, it can never be put right. If a person filled many roles in your life, as my life mate did for me, then all those needs go unmet. And grief is not just about sorrow. It's about anger, fear, depression, loneliness, despair, and many emotions I have not yet identified.

Grief is also physical. Losing a mate ranks at the very top of stressful situations, and that stress itself causes physiological changes. Sometimes I can barely breathe. I don't sleep well, though that is nothing new. Food nauseates me. I have trouble concentrating, and I am always exhausted—grieving takes an unimaginable amount of energy.

Grief also affects one's self-esteem and identity. He was my focus for so many years. Without that focus to give my life meaning, who am I? How do I find meaning, or at least a reason to continue living? The irony of this particular aspect of my grief is that I never wanted to be so involved with anyone. I always thought I was independent. And perhaps I once was and will be again, but apparently I haven't been for many years.

Because of all these different aspects of grief, grief is ever changing, so one can never get a handle on it, at least not for a long while. And grief grows the further one gets from the loved one's death because you see more of the person's life. In my case, the man he was at thirty, at thirty-five, at forty, are all gone now too. Which is another aspect of grief I had never considered: The sheer goneness of the person.

During my mate's last years, I'd started doing things on my own, such as finding a new life and friends online, and I thought I was doing well in my aloneness. But there is a vast difference between being alone with someone and being alone with aloneness. As William Cowper said: *How sweet, how passing sweet, is solitude! But grant me still a friend in my retreat, Whom I may whisper, Solitude is sweet.*

That is one more thing for me to mourn—the friend in my retreat. He is gone. And solitude is no longer sweet. Do I have the courage to grow old alone? The courage to *be* old alone when the time comes? I don't know.

Grief changes a person in ways I cannot yet fathom, but one's nature does not change, and I always tended toward solitude. Perhaps someday I will welcome the solitariness, or at least come to terms with it

Until then, I will continue to find a reason to get up each day. And always, I will miss him.

Day 25, **Grief Journal**

I went to a grief support group yesterday. I wanted to find out how to survive this trauma. They couldn't tell me but, since most of them had endured many months of grief, I learned that it is possible to survive. Many of them felt they hadn't done enough for their dying mates or that they hadn't done it right. Perhaps in these situations there is no "right." There is just "do."

Today I feel as if I'll be able to come to an accommodation with Jeff's death. I will never be okay with it—it's not for me to say it was okay for him to die—but I will be able to get on with my life. It will be good to get out from under the weight of his illness and unhappiness. I have enough of my own unhappiness to contend with.

What did I bring to his life? All the shared emotion of his last months, our reconnection, the reemergence of his sweet self showed me that at rock bottom he cared for me and loved me as much as I loved him. I'm glad I'll be able to remember the bad times, too. I'd hate to revere him in memory, giving him a perfection he never had while alive— it would be a disservice to remember him as he never was. Though, truly, with a few breaks, with good health, with a bit of success, he could have grown into that god-like being I glimpsed when I met him. He really did shine with goodness and vitality back then. So radiant.

He'd never had it easy, but how dreadful it must have been for him that last year—growing so weak, losing his sight and his hearing, knowing he was dying, not understanding why his brain wasn't functioning properly, knowing that nothing would ever work out right.

We always wanted the best for each other, but it didn't seem to be enough. Did we give us the best we had . . .

I just got interrupted—a phone call from Jeff's hospice nurse. She called to see how I was doing, and there went my calm and acceptance. Back to weeping and wailing. Damn it!! I miss him. I wish I could have had more of the radiant man he used to be and less of the person his brain metastases turned him into. I wish I were half the woman I thought I was. I wish . . . oh, crap. What good does wishing do? I'll just have to grow up and learn to live with what is.

Day 26, **Dear Jeff,**

I miss your presence in my life. At times I grieve for you, but right now I'm grieving for me. I'm sorry for making your death about me, but I am the only one in the room. Remember a month or so ago when we were talking about your dying, and I started telling you my fears about the future? I felt bad since you didn't have a future, and I apologized for making your dying about me. You said, "There are two of us in this room." Well, now there aren't. There is only me. I did not want you dead even though there were times I wished your suffering (and mine) were over. Well, you're at peace now (at least, I hope you are). Maybe someday I will be at peace, too.

It just dawned on me that in a way, it's still "our" life though I'm the only one left to carry on. I hope I can get over this absolutely breath-sucking pain so that you can be part of my life without the agony and stress. Maybe then I can smile instead of cry when I remember you.

I got a call from your hospice nurse yesterday, and she said she didn't think we were aware of how much we loved each other. How could we not have known? But what we had didn't feel like love. After a few brief years of hope and happiness, our love was sublimated by the constraints of your growing ill health. It seemed that our cosmic love devolved into the prosaic things of life: cooking meals, doing errands, struggling to keep our retail business alive. And then it devolved further into simply surviving. Getting through the days as best as we could. We always knew we had a deep connection, though we never understood it and at times we both railed against it in our struggle to maintain our own identities, but we took that connection for granted. And what is that connection if not love?

When one of us returned from a trip, we'd hold each other tightly as if we'd never let go. We did let go, though. I threw you away, or rather life did. Perhaps I did the right thing by taking you to the hospice care center, but I'll never forgive myself for letting the nurse talk me into it. And yet, you couldn't swallow unless you were standing, and you didn't have the strength to stand, even with my help. Your end time looms large in my thoughts, though it was so short considering the whole of our lives. If I ever stop writing you, know that you are always in my heart, my mind, the very fabric of my being. What I am, what I will become is due so much to you that you will always be with me, a part of me.

I love you.

Day 27, **Grief Journal**

I realized something today—Jeff was lucid enough at the time we made the decision for him to go to the hospice care center, that if he truly did not want to go, he would have refused. His plaintive remark, "I don't want to go. We have a good life here. We're doing okay, aren't we? I'm not ready for you to throw me away," seems now not so much a refusal to go but a statement of regret. He knew it was the end, but didn't want it to be.

I hope I'm right about this, because I cannot bear to think I deprived him of one more day of living, of lucidity. It really did crush my heart to take him to the care center. I never got to talk with him again—he was in a drug-induced coma for the last five days of his life. I think he was at peace the final two days, though. All the time he was there, his breathing sounded like moaning, and I worried that he was in pain, but during his next-to-last day he exhaled a few melodious-sounding breaths, as if he wanted to reassure me he was okay.

He once told me that if it ever came to his being in a facility, he didn't want me to visit, but how could I not? Even though the care center was sixty-five miles away, I went there every day, but I left early enough so I could get home before dark. The irony is he went there so I could get some rest, but I never did sleep those nights. I was too worried about him.

His last night, Friday night, I didn't go home. A few

snowflakes fell and I used that as an excuse to stay. Also, I was restless, sensing the end was near. So I waited.

Around 1:30 in the morning, his breathing changed. Became harsher. I went to his side, said it was okay for him to leave, that I would be all right. At 1:40, he took a breath. His Adam's apple bobbed once. Twice. And then he was dead. I kissed him by the side of his mouth. Waited a few minutes before I went to get the nurse. I like that I got to tell them he was gone rather than have them tell me.

They cleaned him, though there was nothing to clean. Nor was there a smell.

I didn't cry. Just sat and waited for the funeral director, then I left. The highway was dry, but about halfway home, I hit a patch of black ice. Went careening, around and around, back and forth, totally out of control. I thought I was going to die, but oddly, I never left the road. The car finally came to a halt facing the wrong way on the highway. I was fine. So was the car. I remember wondering if Jeff had stopped by on his way out of this world to leave me a final reminder to be careful, or maybe he was shaking his ghostly head, thinking that after his being gone only two hours, I was already getting careless.

He always worried that I wasn't careful enough. I'm trying to be careful. Trying to take care of myself. I hope he's taking care of himself.

Day 29, **Grief Journal**

Today I feel more like I expected to feel—sad, lonely, empty—without the agonizing grief and horrendous pain that's been with me the past few weeks. Of course, my mind has been elsewhere as I've tried to figure out what of our stuff to keep and what to get rid of. Still, for the four-week anniversary of Jeff's death, I'm a lot calmer than I've been.

I hope eventually I can forget the horror of his death and just be glad we were able to forgive each other, find renewed closeness, say good-bye. I don't want to molder in grief for the rest of my life. My suffering will not mitigate his. I really do think a lot of my "grief work" was done before his death.

He helped by encouraging me to try new things, to go off on adventures by myself. As hard as these weeks have been, they would have been so much worse if I hadn't already started taking baby steps into the rest of my life while I had the cushion of his presence.

Life is so damn unfair. Almost insanely unfair. I hope, in some small way, I made a difference in his life. I hope, if we were ever able to meet again, he could say I was good for him. It seems as if our lives crossed for such a short while before they started to diverge, and now the divergence is irrevocable. I have a hunch as the years pass I'll forget most of the ups and downs of our life, our complicated relationship, this horrendous feeling of amputation, but I'll always remember that I loved him, and that at the end, we recommitted ourselves to each other.

Day 30, **Grief Journal**

I spent all day packing. I'm only going through the things I know I want, the rest I'll deal with when I feel more able to cope. I'm keeping way more of Jeff's things than I planned, but much of it I can't get rid of yet, like his baseball bat and mitt. I'm keeping his video tapes, even the ones I'll never watch. They represent a lot of his time. (I originally wrote "life" then substituted "time," but "life" is also correct. Perhaps time is life?)

I thought I'd gone through the worst of my grief. I've been working so hard getting things packed that I didn't have much time to cry, but when I finally stopped working because of exhaustion, I really HURT. It felt like he had died all over again. Crying didn't help, so I wailed. I hyperventilated. I SCREAMED. I thought I screamed loud enough to wake the dead, but Jeff did not answer me.

I'm not looking forward to going through Jeff's "effects" as he called them. If he didn't have that excruciating pain toward the end (they say cancer in the bone is about the worst possible pain), he would have cleared everything out as he'd planned, but now it's for me to do. Just not today. I'm screamed out.

I found a quote on his bedside table: "Death is the portal to hell, but for some people it is the way out rather than the way in."

I'm glad he's no longer trapped in his personal hell, but I'll never be glad he's out of my life. At least I had him when I needed him. We had all those years of talking, thinking, reading, evaluating, searching for the truth of history and of life. I would like his continued counsel. But I don't *need* it. At least I tell myself that.

Do I have a fate, a purpose? It does seem as if my life is a quest for truth, for understanding, but what's the point? I suppose the journey is the point, but still, at the end of a quest story, the hero returns with the magic elixir. She has a purpose for what she's gone through. Do I? Or is my brain conning me into believing there is purpose to my life? But what about Jeff? What was his purpose? I'll never understand why such a good man had to suffer.

Day 31, **Grief Journal**

Have I mentioned my screaming? After packing the past couple of days, it was the only way to release the incredible pain and tension. I truly did not know I had this much passion bottled up in me. I thought I was a stoic, and would not (could not?) feel much grief.

Today is the "versary" of his death—one month—and I'm no closer to accepting it now than I was then, but I am getting things done, so that is progress. The stuff I'm keeping is in storage, and all I'm left with is the mess of a shattered togetherness and lots of pain.

I do not want my life to be so completely entwined with another's ever again. I need to find ME, the me that exists separately from everyone else, the core me. She will take care of me. I just have to let go and let her do it. Perhaps that's what some of this screaming is about—releasing all the old ties, not just to Jeff and my/our hopes, but to myself. Maybe these are the screams of a new creature being birthed.

I get weirdly mystical when I spend too much time alone, but these mental meanderings could have a bit of truth in them. I hope I will make something of myself. I hope as I move forward that I can be spontaneous, a bit bold, curious, less careless, and more joyful. I hope I can accept without guilt any gifts life brings my way. Maybe my life with Jeff was spring training for the rest of my life, which means there will be happiness and probably pain. But to what end? Just an end?

In a strange way, grief is Jeff's final gift to me. It will change me, perhaps free me. If I come out of this a better person, all the pain will be worth it. But however it turns out, I'd still prefer Jeff alive, well, happy. I wish I could see him one more time, but even if he came back for a moment to talk to me or hug me, that moment, however precious, would become just another memory. And if all we end up with is memories of someone, well . . . I already have those.

Day 32, Blog Post, **I am a One-Month Grief Survivor**

I have survived my first month of grieving. I'm surprised it was so hard, and I'm surprised I survived it (at times my lungs stopped working and my heart felt as if it would burst with all the pain) but in the world of grief, a month isn't much. Still, I've come a long way. I can look to the future, though I know the best way to deal with that future is to deal with each day as it comes—thinking of living the rest of my life without my mate makes me sick to my stomach.

And I have moments when I can stand outside my grief and see the process for what it is. Grief is an enormous undertaking (I hesitated using the word "undertaking" since it's so close to "undertaker," but it's a good analogy because grief is, to a certain extent, facing the death of a part of you). Grief involves physical, emotional, psychological, spiritual, and in my case, geographical changes. Grief rocks you to the very depths of your being—a soul quake. Grief changes your sense of self, your sense of your place in the world. Grief affects your self-esteem. There is only one other experience of such immensity—falling in love.

I have come to realize hate is not the opposite of love, grief is. Grief encompasses all the wild emotions, the life-changing experiences, the immensity of love, but in reverse. Falling in love with the man I was to spend decades with and grieving for him are the bookends of our life—not my life, my life will continue, though changed—but our life, the life we shared.

I wonder sometimes if I'm going to change out of all recognition. I've gone through so many life-changing experiences in the past year that I no longer know who I am.

Will he recognize me if we ever meet again? Will he be proud of what I become? I guess that is part of the future, not of this day. And right now, this day is all I can handle.

Second Month

Day 33, **Grief Journal**

I'm tired of pushing against the juggernaut of fate. No matter how hard I tried, nothing I did made a bit of difference. Jeff still died. Maybe it's better to let life flow, to try to accept what comes, but isn't the point of being human to try to make a difference? To try to change what is?

I am slowly (or rapidly—how the heck do I know? Time has ceased to have meaning.) being dissociated from life and I need to try to reconnect somehow. Maybe after we move, I'll feel less disembodied. After *we* move? Ouch. It's going to take a long time to remember I am no longer part of a "we". Well, I guess in a way "we" *are* moving. He's so much a part of me, I'm not sure anymore how much of me is me and how much of me is him. I'll have to figure it out, I suppose, so I can get on with my life.

Toward the end, Jeff told me that everything would come together for me after he was gone, though I'm not really sure what he meant by that.

I'd like to accomplish something with my life and my writing. I'd like to write a book that touches people's hearts, that makes a difference in their lives. It feels as if I've been coasting for years. Not waiting for Jeff to die, but just . . . waiting. Now it's time to do something. But what? For now, grieving is about all I can do.

I read something recently: *nothing happens and then everything happens.* During the past couple of years, nothing seemed to happen, but then after his diagnosis, everything happened. So many changes! As painful as they are, maybe the changes in my life will be good for me in a spinachy sort of way: not what I want, not what I choose, but necessary for my well-being.

Day 34, **Grief Journal**

Everything seems to be falling apart all at once. The roof

leaks, the kitchen faucet drips, my car needs new tires, the engine is losing oil, the bushings for the stick shift need to be replaced, the timing skips, my jaw infection flared up, the internet signal got lost for most of the night, and it snowed for two days. It seems as if together Jeff and I held back the tide of entropy, and now it's slamming into me with great force. If I survive this—and I will, drat it!—I should come out of it stronger.

I know these problems are not that great, and normally I could take them in stride, but right now everything over-whelms me. I'm trying to take things one step at a time.

Trying to get through the days one minute at a time.

I sound calm, but in truth I am furious about the whole damn situation. And sad and empty and lonely and a thousand other emotions that fall under the heading of grieving.

Damn it! Damn it! Damn it!

Day 35, **Grief Journal**

Jeff was so smart. How can that intelligence be gone? I try to make sense of his death, but how do you make sense of something senseless?

The hospice social worker says my grief has been so intense it's as if I'm in my sixth month of grieving. A minister friend says I've handled it better than anyone he knows. So what? Jeff is still dead. No matter how I handle the situation, it won't bring him back. This is the reality I have to live with, like it or not. And I don't like it. But I always return to the same thought: given the circumstances of his life, I know he's glad to be out of it. Not much comfort, but it's all I have.

Day 36, **Grief Journal**

I can't see this page for tears. I still am not getting a grip on my grief, though I am able to do things and to focus. Grief comes more as waves now, sometimes when I am least expecting it.

I'm sad for me, and I feel sorry for me. I feel sorry he's

not in my life anymore, and I feel sorry that his ill health stole a normal life from us. I feel sorry that . . . well, hell, I just feel sorry. The world has changed in some unidentifiable way. He stepped off the earth, and now everything is askew. Unbalanced.

No one ever cared for me the way Jeff did. He listened and he heard what I said. He was always present for me. Well, except for the past few years, which is why I so often felt that no one ever had time for me, but that simply is not true. He had *years* for me. Decades. The thought that he'll never be here for me again grieves me beyond all comprehension. I hope I was always there for him. I know I was there for the end when he really needed someone.

Every year I live will diminish his presence in my life. He looms large now because we were together for more than half my years, but if I live to be as old as my father is, Jeff and I will have been together only a third of my life.

The world is not such a good place (not that it ever was) without him. I remember when I met him how the world suddenly became brighter and more hopeful. If he were in the world, it couldn't be all bad. If he were in the world, I wasn't out of place. Well, he is no longer in the world, and I feel totally out of place.

Perhaps, as they say, everything happens for the best, but whose best? Was it best that he suffered? Was it best that he died? Was it best that I'm left to live out my life alone? Could it be best in some bizarre way I cannot yet imagine.

Things generally happen "for the best" after the fact. Our brains seek order, so we look back to see how we ended up where we are, and we say, "yes, everything happened for the best," though it's simply our trickster brains at work.

But . . . just for today, I will act as if everything is happening for the best.

Day 37, Grief Journal

I am very depressed right now. The damn jaw infection isn't going away. I can't stop crying. I get worse the more I get used to Jeff being gone. What right do I have to get used to his being dead? It's like a negation of his life.

It's amazing how life changes from one second to the next. Jeff didn't want me to have to take care of him. He didn't want me to have to watch him die. I think he'd planned to get rid of his stuff, then take off and go somewhere to die alone, but that option evaporated between one heartbeat and the next. He bent down to pick up a paper, and that was it. No more choices but how long to endure the bone-crushing pain before he sought relief.

Death came as quickly. One breath, one bob of his Adam's apple, and his life was gone. And mine changed forever.

There is no way to find anything positive about this situation, no way to make it come out right. This is the true coming of age—this experience of irrevocable loss. Of living with something that cannot be changed. Frankly, I want my naiveté back.

Day 39, **Grief Journal**

I detest this roller coaster of emotions, though it's not a roller coaster since there are no ups, only downs. It's more of a side-to-side shimmy.

I woke this morning in tears. I am still depressed. Still feel way too much mental and physical pain. Still scream for Jeff.

Someone suggested that I concentrate on the enrichment he brought to my life and less on my loss. It's too soon for that, though—even good memories bring about a spate of grief. I hate feeling so maimed. I hate feeling that there is no one just for me any more. I hate feeling so damn alone.

At the grief group yesterday a woman said she wished her divorced daughter would find someone to grow old with. As if that's all that was necessary—to find someone. I did have someone to grow old with, and now I don't. Even if I come out of this okay, Jeff will still be dead, so how is that okay? Damn it! This is not the way our lives were supposed to be!

I've been reading old *Reader's Digests*, and boy, are those enough to scare a person half to death—stories of awful diseases, dreadful problems of aging, terrible accidents, all the horrors the world has to offer. And from now on, whatever happens to me, I'll have to deal with it alone.

We always tried to be safe, to be healthy, and still, Jeff got sick. A mutual acquaintance said to me, "How could Jeff have let himself get sick like that?" What??!! As if Jeff chose to get cancer. Sheesh. A woman at the grief group mentioned that this county has a higher than normal rate of cancer. Could that have been a factor? Even if it is, it doesn't change anything.

I hope Jeff didn't suffer too much at the very end.

I miss him. I miss working with him, talking with him, watching movies with him, laughing with him. I miss our shared hopes for a better future. It's a good thing I have so much to do—getting my car ready for the trip, getting ready for the yard sale—otherwise I'd just sit around feeling even sorrier for myself.

I have to steel myself to go on. I will not molder for the rest of my life. If I'm going to be here on Earth, I want to live, laugh, love. But not yet. I'm not ready to let go of my grief. It's all I have left of Jeff.

Day 40, **Dear Jeff,**

I wasn't going to write you this morning since I had to get up early to take my car in for some work, but I woke early and am lying here thinking about you. Are you in a better place? Considering your life, even oblivion would be a better place. I wish we could meet again, but the only way to do that is after I'm dead, too, and then it wouldn't matter if oblivion is all there is—I'd be oblivious to the pain of not seeing you again. I'd also be done with this anguish. From what I hear, this pain of your being gone will always be with me, though never quite as raw as it is now. I know you'd never wish this on me, but that's the way things are.

Did you feel burdened by me the past couple of years? Did you worry about what would happen to me after you were gone? (I know you did!) I'm sorry for that. I'm sorry for so many things, even those that were not my fault, such as your ill health. I am truly glad you went first. I'd hate to think of your enduring grief for me along with everything else you've suffered.

Did I tell you I'm thinking of keeping your car? I'm getting rid of so much of our stuff—the extra electronics, books, tools—but I'm not ready to let go of that last vestige of you.

I don't feel good about leaving here, but I don't feel good about staying, either. I'd always have that sick feeling when I entered the house—the feeling that something is dreadfully wrong, which it is.

I wish I told you more often that I loved you.

Day 43, **Grief Journal**

On Wednesday I took my car to the mechanic to get it ready for the trip, on Thursday, I took Jeff's car to get the brakes fixed, then yesterday I had the first day of the yard sale. Spent most of last evening crying and screaming. "Grief work" they call it. It's sickening (literally) to be dismantling our lives. Sickening to think of leaving here, leaving Jeff behind.

My time with Jeff wasn't always "quality" time in that we were out of sync the past couple of years (no wonder, what with his dying) but I have learned one thing. ALL time with a loved one is quality time. Time is the currency of love. It's not so much what you feel as what you do. It's having time for someone, being present for him.

I do okay while writing in this journal. I can write rationally about Jeff, our past and my future, but when I'm in the throes of anguish, I'm anything but rational. This whole experience makes me feel unbalanced. Well, I am un-balanced. When Jeff stepped off the world, he unbalanced it, unbalanced me. I have to find balance and do it on my own—I can't expect anyone else to balance me and my world.

Well, gotta go get ready for another yard sale day. The worst part comes not from selling our stuff for pocket change, but from seeing all the couples picking over the shards of our life. If I'd known that the only ones stopping would be older couples, I might not have put myself through this. It's too difficult. Reminds me that I am no longer half of a couple. That I have no one to grow old with. No one to be with.

I won't cry.

At least not until I'm alone tonight.

Day 45, Grief Journal

The yard sale was mostly a waste. I made enough to pay for hauling away the rest of the stuff. I still have Jeff's things to clear out—his clothes, his papers, his "effects"—but I just don't have the energy to tackle the job.

I've finally gotten off the go/stay seesaw. I understand that whatever I decide will be the right decision, so I'm going to stick to my original plan. I don't know why I've been making such a big deal about it—my father really does need someone to stay with him, so I don't have much of a choice. Besides, it's a change, which I need, and it's what Jeff wanted me to do—he worried about leaving me behind. The night before he died, I told him I'd go stay with my father, and I think that helped him find release. Strangely, I hadn't been worried about my future—I really did think I'd be okay after he was gone. Sheesh. Crying and wailing and screaming are not my idea of being okay. Jeff dealt with his infirmities and agony with such stoicism that he'd probably be ashamed of me, but it's the only way I can survive the sheer animal pain of it all.

What a ridiculous mess my life is in. What a ridiculous mess my mind is in. There just doesn't seem to be any point to anything. Maybe the point is there is no point. You just do something and see what happens. So, I'll be leaving in three weeks. Then we'll see if anything develops.

Day 46, Dear Jeff,

I miss you, miss being able to talk with you. I haven't heard from you, but why you'd respond to my letters, I don't know. You probably don't feel like talking to me after all my resistance to your "lectures." I just did not want to hear what you had to say about your death. Did not want to think of my life after you were gone.

Now that I know how incredibly difficult grieving is, I'd give anything to hear one more of those lectures about what to do when you're dead. I now understand how worried you were about me. I thought you were being paternalistic. I thought you didn't trust me to live right, to do what needed to be done, to be careful, but you were concerned for me, trying to prepare me for a world in which you would not be present, leaving me with words that would have to last the rest of my life.

I wish I had understood the situation, but the irony is that until one has experienced such a "loss" (cripes, I hate that word) and the ensuing grief, there is no way to comprehend the finality of dying. I still can't comprehend it, can't comprehend the ramifications, but I can experience the grief of it. I tell myself I'm glad to do this for you—if I had died first, you would have had to experience it, and I am saving you from that.

I truly do not understand the depth of my pain. Some of it is feral, animalistic, from somewhere so deep inside I've never been there. I feel as if my psyche is a bloody stump where you have been ripped away. Do you feel the same? I sure hope not. I can only go on if I know you are at peace.

I love you immeasurably.

Day 47, **Grief Journal**

I had a curious notion yesterday. I've been finding comfort in the thought that Jeff is at peace, but what if he isn't? What if there is some sort of life after death and he's feeling as split apart as I am? According to one expert, there could be problems depending on how codependent the person was. Whatever that means. I thought a relationship was about being dependent on each other, and we were. That's what this past year has been about—untwinning our lives so we could go our separate ways. That's why this grief has shocked me so much—I thought we had untwinned.

I can see that people would have questions about codependency considering how bereft I am without Jeff and how lost I feel, but when he was alive, we were never obsessed with each other, though we were connected in so many ways. We were friends, life mates, and business partners. We always wanted what was best for the other. We helped each other grow. We never expected the other to fix our individual problems, though we often took each other's advice. We didn't cling, demand, or base our relationship on unrealistic expectations. Together we provided a safe environment where each of us could be ourselves. And we supported each other any way we could.

Long-term illness, however, does skew a relationship. Over the years, our world kept getting smaller and smaller, trapping us in a terrible situation where neither his nor my needs were being met. To that extent, his death freed me, but for what?

Day 49, **Dear Jeff,**

It's been seven interminable weeks since I watched you die. I hope you are at peace. At first I felt terrible for you that you're gone, now I feel terrible for me that I'm not.

Ours wasn't always a good life, but we did make the best of it. I love that we never stopped trying. I love that we talked so much. I love that we cared for each other even at those times we didn't particularly like each other. I love your smile, your intelligence, your courage, your determination to do things your way (as infuriating as that sometimes was). I love your wisdom. I love that you shared your life with me. I love that you tried to prepare me for when you'd be gone.

It was hard when you pulled away from me this past year. Did you not want to talk about what you were going through? Did you not want to bother me? Were you afraid of burdening me? Did you get tired of my resistance to the thought of your dying?

I can't comprehend that year, not what you went through, not my insistence on living despite your dying. We still

41

managed to have some good times. The trip to the Black Canyon was magnificent. I hate looking at that photo I took of you, though—it tears me apart. You look fragile—I had no idea you lost so much weight. I remember how hard it was for you to walk. And still you lived seven more months

Until death came for you, we always shared everything. If anything good happens to me now, how do I share it with you?

I'm assuming I'm going to be okay, otherwise you wouldn't have left me. As if you had a choice. But maybe you did. Maybe you really were through with life.

Will we meet again? Will you recognize me? Will you be proud of me? At the risk of sounding patronizing: I am proud of you. I love you, miss you, wish you all the best.

Day 52, **Grief Journal**

I haven't done well cleaning out Jeff's stuff. Done well? Done not at all! Cleared out some magazines, but nothing else. It just tears me up (rips me up *and* makes me cry) when I catch sight of something of his—this morning it was a slipper.

Still trying to figure out what to do with his car. I fixed the brakes, but now it needs new tires. Is it worth the expense? Probably not.

I think (hope) I'm getting to the point where I can accept Jeff's and my shared life—at least my part in it—as "That's the way it was. Period." I don't want regrets, don't want to think and rethink what happened, don't want to blame myself for any misunderstandings. We both coped the only way we could.

Part of me still doesn't comprehend that he's dead. Part of me comprehends in spurts, and when the truth washes over me, the pain is overwhelming.

I miss him, miss our life, miss the dreams we had.

Day 53, **Dear Jeff,**

When are you coming back? I have a vague feeling in the far recesses of my mind that this is some sort of test. It will soon be over and things will return to normal. But what's normal—you suffering, you in pain? You've wanted out of that life for a long time, and now you have it. Your body can no longer betray you. Your cancer-ridden brain can no longer let you down. You're free. I wish I could be happy for you, but I still feel your pain and unhappiness (surrogate sufferer that I am) along with my own. I have a hunch as I let go, first of your pain and then of mine, I'll remember only that we loved each other.

We seldom used the word "love" because the connotations of that word didn't seem to fit with our relationship. It seemed such a paltry description for the connection we had. We just were. And now we're not. I can't get a handle on that. I wish I could celebrate our shared life, but I haven't reached that point yet.

My grief support group accused me of trying too hard to hurry the grief process. Supposedly, I can't heal (as if your dying was an illness) if I try to skim past the pain, but I don't see the point of all this mourning. (Supposedly mourning is the outward expression of grief, but grief and mourning mean the same to me.) I sometimes wonder how you would handle it if our positions were reversed. But I do know how. You felt so terrible for me those times I was sick that my death—especially if under such cruel circumstances as yours—would leave you feeling as awful as I feel.

I'm going to be glad to leave this house. I just wish we were starting a new life together, that we were going somewhere filled with hope. My hopes died with you, but I hope (Ah! A hope!) that someday I will find new hopes.

I miss you, Jeff. Adios, compadre.

Day 54, **Grief Journal**

I feel lost without Jeff. I have no one who cares for me in a daily, practical manner; no one to tell the inconsequential and not-so-inconsequential happenings of my day; no one to notice if I get up in the morning.

I do get up. There is still much that needs to be done, though to be honest, I'm not doing it. Can't gather the courage or the strength or the energy to go through Jeff's things. Can't gather the desire, either, since disposing of his things will take me further into my life alone, and I'm not ready to go off without him.

I'm beginning to understand how his absence will affect the rest of my life. I will always miss him, always have periods of bleakness, always have a hole in my heart, always have an undercurrent of sadness even in happy times.

I finally decided what to do with his car. I'm going to donate it to hospice. I let them have Jeff. Might as well let them have his car. They will come pick it up after I'm gone so I'll be able to drive away as if I'm just going on another trip, leaving him behind to await my return.

I'm crying. Didn't know I still had so many tears left in me. Can someone drown in tears? I still cry for hours every day. Sometimes minutes at a time at frequent intervals, sometimes hours at a time after long intervals of not crying.

My screaming has abated, though, mostly because I don't have the energy for it.

I know I should be grateful for having had Jeff as long as I did, and I am, but I have so many years left to live alone. One consolation, as a person ages, the years go by quickly.

Day 55, **Grief Journal**

I cleaned out Jeff's "effects" today. Cried the entire day, not just when I was working. I have never felt such soul-wrenching agony. I didn't want to block out the pain—don't want to risk becoming hardened and unable to feel—but I sure as hell don't want to *ever* go through anything like that again.

The only good thing about living the worst day of your life is that every day afterward, no matter how bad, will be better than that day.

Day 58, **Dear Jeff,**

Did you hear me talking to you last night? I didn't want to go to sleep, so I talked to you most of the night—told you what's going on, told you my fears, told you I can finally accept that you're in a better place. (To paraphrase Kate in *A Spark of Heavenly Fire*: even oblivion is better than what you had to deal with.)

Cleaning out your things was like a protracted memorial service, a remembrance of your life. The work and my pain was my final gift to you. I'll never be able to do anything else for you, so I'm glad I could do that one last service.

I'm trying to remember everything you told me, but I can't recall if you ever told me how to survive once you were gone. We talked about places I could go, but did we ever talk about how I should live? How to find a desire to live? How to deal with the pain?

My pain is muted today, but I feel it in all of me—maybe I always will, and in a way, I'll gladly accept it. It will be a reminder that I once loved, I once was loved. A reminder that dreams don't always come true, but a soul connection endures.

Adios, compadre. Rest well.

Day 59, Blog Post, **Misconceptions About Grief**

I attended the grief support group today, my sixth time for that particular group, but I'll need to find another group when I get relocated. It's good to be able to talk about my grief and my lost mate without fear of boring people. And I am beginning to fear that very thing. It seems as if I'm standing in place while the rest of the world moves on, which adds to my feeling of isolation. I had no problem talking or blogging about my grief at the beginning—it was new to me and to those I encountered. But now that I know I could still be dealing with these same feelings long after everyone else has forgotten—it could be a year, perhaps even two (and sometimes, or so I've heard, the second year is worse than the first as the reality settles into one's soul) – I've been hesitant to mention my bereftness lest I incur impatience in others. Or even worse, lest I seem as if I'm milking my personal tragedy for attention.

I asked the group today how they handled the situation (the others were almost two years into their bereavement), and they said they stopped talking about their loss except to the group. To everyone else they'd use phrases such as "I'm coping," or "I'm doing okay all things considered." When I asked if I should hide my grief, the counselor said no—too many people hide their grief, and it's important to let others know what grief is, how it affects a person and her life.

So here, on my blog, I'm going to continue talking about the experience, continue to share what I learn. Grief is so not what I thought it was. I assumed from what I'd read and seen that the bereft felt sad and lonely, perhaps empty and lost. It is that and so much more. It affects us physically, spiritually, mentally. It creates a void in the body that disease, accidents, and violence hasten to fill. (The death rate for a person grieving her mate increases by 27%.) It affects our self-esteem and our sense of place in the universe. It makes us question our values and the meaning of our lives. It changes us forever, and we need a long time to integrate the loss and pain into our personal identity.

There are many misconceptions about grief such as:

- All losses are the same
- All bereaved people grieve in the same way
- It takes two weeks to three months to get over your grief
- When grief is resolved, it never comes up again
- It is better to put painful thoughts out of your mind
- Anger should not be part of your grief
- You will have no relationship with your loved one after death
- It is best to put the memories of your loved one in the past and go on with your life
- It is best to get involved and stay busy so there is no space to feel pain
- Crying doesn't solve anything

I'm not sure about the last misconception. Crying really doesn't seem to solve anything, but it does have a place. Without tears and yes, I admit it, screams, the pain has no place to go but deeper inside. I'm also not sure about having a relationship with my loved one after his death, but I like the idea. I just don't know how to do it. I'll let you know when I figure it out. Or you can let me know. I need all the help I can get.

Day 62, Blog Post, **I Am a Two-Month Grief Survivor**

I have now survived two months without my life mate—not easily and not well, but I have managed to get through all those days, hours, minutes. The absolute worst day, though, was last Thursday. You would think it would have been the day he died, but that was a sadly inevitable day, one I actually had looked forward to. He'd been sick for so long and in such pain, that I was glad he finally let go and drifted away. After he died, I kissed him goodbye then went to get the nurse, who confirmed that he was gone. She called the funeral home, and I sat there in the room with him for two hours until they finally came for him. (They came in an SUV, not a hearse. And they used a red plush coverlet, not a body bag.) I might have cried. I might have been numb. I don't really remember. All I know is that I sat there with him until almost dawn. I couldn't even see his face—they had cleaned him and wrapped him in a blanket—so I just sat there, thinking nothing.

But last Thursday I spent all day cleaning out his closet and drawers, and going through boxes of his "effects." He had planned to do it himself, but right before he could get started, he was stricken with debilitating pain that lasted to the end of his life, and so he left it for me to do. I did know what to do with most things because he had rallied enough to tell me, but still, there were a few items that blindsided me, such as photos and business cards from his first store (where we met). Every single item he owned was emotionally laden, both with his feelings and mine, and I cried the entire time, huge tears dripping unchecked, soaking my collar.

How do you dismantle someone's life? How do you dismantle a shared life? With care and tears, apparently.

A couple of days later I started cleaning out my office (I have to leave the place we lived for the past two decades, as if losing him isn't trauma enough). I didn't expect any great emotional upheaval—it was my stuff after all—but still it turned out to be an emotional day, though nowhere near as catastrophic as Thursday. This is the first move as an adult I will make alone. It will be the first move I ever made with no real hopes, no lightheartedness. I'm going to a place to write and to heal, not to settle down for good. And my mate will not be there.

Part of me is glad to be getting away from this house, this area—our life here started out with such hope and ended in such despair. Part of me feels as if I'm running away from the pain of losing him, but I have a hunch the pain will always be with me. At least I will never again have the agony of clearing out his things. Oh, no! I forgot! I've sent several boxes of his stuff to be stored, the things I cannot yet get rid of. Eventually I will have to dispose of the things I can't use, but perhaps I can wait until it won't be such a traumatic event. I never want to live through another day like last Thursday. I'm surprised I lived through it this time.

Third Month

Day 64, **Dear Jeff,**

My sister just left. She came to clean the house—even brought cleaning supplies and a helper. I thought it was important for me to clear out your things as sort of a memorial service to you, but cleaning the house? Nope. Was glad of the help. Didn't have the energy to do it myself.

My sister said she thought I could be entering the happiest time of my life, which is possible, I suppose. I haven't been happy for a long time. If I could, I'd trade any future happiness just to be with you again. But only as long as you were healthy. Wouldn't want to condemn you to more suffering. I'd forgotten how relieved I was when you died—not for me, but for you. I've let my grief muddle that.

She also said something profound. I said, "If you're right, and I am entering the happiest time of my life, what does that say about my life with Jeff?" She responded, "It doesn't say anything."

That's true, isn't it? Our life existed whole and entire of itself. Whatever happens to me in the future will not change any of it, will not change its importance or its meaning, will not change what you taught me by your life.

You taught me about bravery and determination and finding a reason to keep going even when there is no reason. You taught me about love, and you taught me about living. It's as if I've graduated from school and now have to put everything I learned to good use. Okay, not like school—how many people use everything they learned in school?

I am apprehensive about the future, and hesitant, but there is a part of me that peeks around the grief and feels a touch of excitement at what could lie ahead.

If you're around, I need a favor. I have a pinched nerve in my left shoulder, exacerbated by the horrendous amount of work I did yesterday. Will you rub it for me? Relax it? Take away the pain? I find it odd that I feel pain in the same place you did. If I've somehow subconsciously shouldered your pain, will you help me unshoulder it? It doesn't seem fair to ask since I couldn't help you get rid of your pain, but I am worried about driving in this condition.

Grief is turning me into a baby. Yesterday when I was packing things for my trip, I couldn't find this notebook. I started crying, "I need my letters to Jeff. Where are my letters to Jeff?" Even after I found them, I couldn't stop crying. I've shed buckets of tears—well, cupfuls anyway.

I'm keeping a key to the house for you and a set of your car keys in case you need them. I'm being silly, I know, just as I'm being silly when I cradle your ashes and rock them or when I talk to you or write you, but dang it! I hate that you're gone. I have to do what I can to find comfort.

I hope you don't feel burdened by me, by my neediness. The rehearsals for being alone (the trips I took, the walks, the internet) have done nothing (or not much) to prepare me for my aloneness. I'm still sick to my stomach, as if the world unbalanced when you stepped off, but I have moments now when I don't feel it as much. So the queasiness, too, will pass. But you will still be gone. Damn it!

Day 65, **Grief Journal**

I'm not sure if I'm getting any benefit from keeping this journal, but I've managed to survive this far, so it must be doing some good. I talk to Jeff more now than I did at the beginning (the beginning of my grief, that is). Will probably become the crazy old lady who walks down the street muttering to a person who isn't there.

It really was a joy having someone to converse with about everything and anything. Jeff and I used to talk from morning to night, then continue the discussion when we woke the next day.

I loved the way we argued. He'd state his position and I'd state mine (or vice versa). If we couldn't agree, we'd walk away (sometimes in a huff, sometimes in frustration). The next day, he'd bring up the subject again, conceding that I was right. Of course, by then I'd have mulled over what he said, and I'd concede that he was right. So we were back where we started. The best thing about it is I knew he'd thought about what I said, he hadn't just blown me off by walking away.

I don't want to idealize him—I want to remember the man he was—but for much of our lives together, I did idealize him. Thought he was so very special.

When I met him, my life became full of wonderful possibilities. And now? Not so much.

Day 66, Blog Post, **Tempest Tossed**

I'm going to be without the internet for a couple of weeks, so don't worry if I don't post for a while.

I'd always planned to follow the conventional wisdom and not move for at least a year after my life mate died, but here I am, two months into my grief, and I am moving—not by choice, but circumstance. Right now I'm rattling around in an empty house, filling it with tears. Though I'm mostly moved and packed and the house cleaned, I am not ready to go—it is way too soon. But even if I could stay, it wouldn't change anything. My mate would still be dead. And I'd still be homeless—he was my home, not this house.

Despite my declaration (after having to throw away so much stuff these past weeks) that I would never buy anything again (except electronics) I did buy a new camera (a cheap little thing, but it works, and besides, a digital camera is electronic, right?). I took pictures of this place today: our cars parked next to each other, the bushes we planted that enclose the house and give it privacy, the hybrid bush/tree I borrowed for my novel *Light Bringer* (which will always be tinged with sadness for me since he never got to help proof it, never got to see it). I don't know if I will ever be able to look at the photos without weeping, but at least I have them.

From what I've heard about the loss of a mate, as hard as the first months are, the second year of grieving sometimes is even worse. I cannot imagine that. But then, I never could have imagined the pain I am feeling now. I don't know why, but occasionally the loss hits me anew, as if it just happened. Which is what I am feeling today. And, apparently, that too is normal. It still happens to some people even a decade later.

Our life together—his and mine—is receding, even in memory, as if it's a fantasy, a dream, a mirage. When he was alive, the past always seemed present. Now it seems so very past (passed?). That's one more loss to add to so many.

I feel tempest-tossed. As if I am unmoored. Swept away on an emotional storm. Besides all the other emotions that beset me, I find I panic easily. While cleaning my car, getting ready for the trip, I took up the mat on the floor of the driver's side and discovered . . . rusted-out holes. Yikes. I'm about to go on a long trip with holes in my car where my feet rest? Panic! There is no such thing as ER for car bodies as I discovered after a spate of phone calls, so when I calmed down, I patched the floorboard using aluminum foil, metal tape (way cool stuff!), oven liners, and cardboard. Should last as long as my car.

I'm sure I will be okay, eventually. Just not yet.

Day 67, **Dear Jeff,**

Did you have a good night? Are you sleeping? Do you sleep? Do you still exist somewhere as yourself or has your energy been reabsorbed into the universe? I think about you constantly—I hope it doesn't bother you that I'm still clinging to you emotionally. I feel unsettled, and I'm having a hard time processing all this—our life together, your death, the end of our shared life.

I keep saying I don't know how to live without you, but I do. The problem is I don't know how to *want* to live without you. No one will ever take your place. No one will ever mean to me what you did, in the way you did.

It seems strange that I'm leaving here. The topic of where I should go caused our few disagreements last year. There were just a few, weren't there? It was such a calamitous year, I no longer know the truth of it.

I look to you for how to be brave. Thank you for that day

you talked to me about courage. You thought it was for you, a way of gathering your courage to face your painful dying, but it was for me—I need to be brave to get through the coming days, months, years.

Adios, compadre. I hope you no longer have need of bravery.

Day 68, **Grief Journal**

Sometimes I think I'm dramatizing this whole situation, making a big deal out of a natural occurrence, then grief swallows me and I know Jeff's death and my reaction to it is real.

I'm almost ready to leave, to start the next phase of my life. Will I be happy as my sister suggested? Will things come together for me as Jeff said? Will I stagnate during this transitional phase or will I find a new creativity, a new focus?

I feel like a fledgling being pushed from the nest with no idea of how to use my wings. Whether I look forward to the change or look back in longing, whether I drag my feet or wing it, I'm leaving here. Alone.

I have many doubts and fears, but despite them, I hope I will run to meet my destiny. And if there is no destiny? If there is no happiness for me? Well, I'll accept whatever comes, both good and bad, with courage.

Day 75, Blog Post, **Yes, I Can**

It seems as if it's been a lifetime since I wrote an article for this blog, and perhaps it has been. I thought my move away from the house I lived for the past two decades with my life mate would be the start of a life change—a real journey. I expected to be different at the end of my trip to my new location than I was at the beginning, but in truth, the change had already begun.

During these past months, I've had so much thrown at me that I was overwhelmed. First my mate's death, then arranging his cremation, packing and storing the stuff I'm going to keep, doing a yard sale, cleaning out his things, disposing of all the detritus one accumulates during a shared life time, preparing for my journey. All this I did alone while dealing with overwhelming grief. During each agonizing step of the way, I'd cry and wail and scream, "I can't do this!" So much pain. So much loss. So much change in such a short time. And I had no idea how to cope.

My last morning at the house, I got up early, cleaned out the few remaining items I'd been using, packed my car, and took one more look around the house. I walked through the rooms, remembering with what hope we had moved there, remembering the good times, remembering the more frequent bad times. Remembering his last hug, his last kiss. His death.

As I was shutting the door, I thought of all that lay ahead of me, and I cried, "I can't do this."

Then, it dawned on me: Yes. I can. Because I did.

I got out my camera and went through the house one last time, taking photos of the empty rooms to prove to myself that all those things I thought I couldn't do, I did.

I know there will still be much for me to have to deal

with—learning how to live without him, learning who I am now that I am not part of a couple, finding a way and a reason to live—and through it all, I might continue to wail, "I can't do this," but the truth is, I can. And that was the real journey, the real discovery. The trip turned out to be just a trip.

Day 76, **Dear Jeff,**

Well, I'm here. Now what? I called our phone number—I wanted to make sure you were okay and to ask you what I'm supposed to do now—but you didn't answer. Please call me and tell me I can come home. Please?

I still can't fathom that you're dead. Still can't fathom your sheer goneness. I have times when I know I'll be okay—after living through your dying and my first two months of grief, I can live through anything. I still feel as if the world is tilted, still hope someday we will be reunited (which takes a leap of faith I do not have).

I always wanted to know the truth, to face reality without the buffer of unfounded hopes, but this is way too much reality for me. I keep thinking that I want you back, but I don't—you've suffered enough. But, if there were any chance of your returning strong, healthy, happy, I'd welcome you in a heartbeat. You know where to find me.

Adios, compadre.

Day 77, **Dear Jeff,**

I hope you are well and not suffering. I hope you ARE. I've set out a few of your things (perpetual calendar, eyeglasses, books). I've progressed to the point where I want to see items that remind me of you. Maybe they will bring me peace instead of pain. Maybe they will help me feel connected to you.

You told me to keep any of your clothes that fit me. If not for your suggestion, I would never have considered it, but I did keep a couple of coats and your hat. Strange to think of life mimicking art. Remember Greg in *A Spark of Heavenly Fire*? He wore his dead father's trench coat and fedora as a tribute to him, and now I wear yours. Looks good on me, too. (Actually, your hat isn't a fedora, it's an Irish walking hat, but the point is still the same.)

A dozen times a day I think of things to tell you, sometimes I even get out of the chair to find you, and then I remember you're gone. As bad as that is, it will be even worse if I forget you.

Can you tell that I am crying?

The days are passing swiftly. We're already into June. I feel as if I am running against time, but there isn't a reason to be concerned about the passing days any more. Or am I missing something? For so long, I had the feeling we were running out of time, and we did run out when you died. The race against death had only one winner. And it wasn't me and it wasn't you.

It seems as if my internal clock was reset at the time of your death, and now my body ticks out the days, weeks, months that you've been gone. Other than that, the passing days mean nothing. Except that I'm growing older, of course.

I haven't figured out what to do with the rest of my life. This is just a way station on my journey, a transitional stage between my life with you and my life alone, and soon I will need to make some decisions. But not now. I'm drifting, trying to live in the day. Thinking of living so many decades without you scares me. Thinking of growing old and feeble scares me. Last night I watched one of the movies you taped. *Pizza My Heart*. Dan Hedaya sure lost his fire. I guess we all do when we get old.

I'd planned to write once I got here, but I have no interest in writing—no focus, no ability to think or create. No interest in much of anything.

I took a walk yesterday. I thought I'd mostly have to walk on suburban streets, but I turned down a nearby road and ended up in the desert. Within half an hour I was out of sight of the city—just me and the desert. It was a lovely day— clear and warm with a brisk breeze. Very peaceful

I hope you're at peace. Adios, compadre. I love you.

Day 78, **Grief Journal**

I've been crying all day and didn't know why until I looked at the calendar and realized it was Saturday. Eleven weeks since he's been gone. How can so much time have passed? How can so little time have passed?

Seems to me I'd better make a friend of pain—I'll always miss Jeff, always grieve for him in some way. I'm feeling sorry for myself, but so what? A major phase of my life is over, and not by my choosing.

During the year before his death, while he died a bit more each day, I insisted on living, on going on with my life. And now? I don't want to go on at all. The years stretch out before me like a psychical desert—harsh, severe, relieved only by an occasional oasis. How does one live a bleak life? Day by endless day, I guess.

It seems as if all I do is wait. Wait for my grief to dissipate a bit. Wait until I'm used to Jeff's being gone. Wait until something happens, preferably something good to balance the pain, (though happiness isn't a requirement for living). I wish I knew what's the point of it all. Once you're dead, does it matter that you were alive? Does the length of your life mean anything?

I miss talking to Jeff. I never felt so alive as when we were volleying ideas. I'll never have that again. Never have him again. There's a chance my life will open up, present opportunities I cannot even imagine, but I keep coming back to the same thing—without Jeff, it won't matter. He was the witness to my life. He gave it meaning by that witnessing. So that's two things I no longer get from Jeff that I'll have to find within myself—"home" and "witness."

Does it matter to Jeff that I witnessed his life? Witnessed his death? He couldn't witness it—he was living it. (Living a death? Sounds oxymoronic.) Either way, he didn't pass unnoticed from this life. I was there. I noticed.

Day 79, **Grief Journal**

I have nothing to say. Feel more blank than bleak. Have no desire to do anything, no desire to start my life over, no desire to figure anything out.

Maybe something will happen. Maybe not. Maybe I'll start caring about something. Maybe not. Maybe I'll start living again—or maybe I already am. Maybe this is living, though it doesn't feel like it.

Day 80, **Grief Journal**

Crying again. Feeling heartbroken. No other word can describe this desolation.

Most of the people in my grief group think they will see their mates again in another life. Some believe their mates are still looking out for them. If there is another life after this one, I don't want to keep Jeff tied to me—I'd like to think he was free, happy, learning, fulfilled, gone to a higher plane, taking his rightful place in the pantheon of radiance. Hanging around me, taking care of me is not the eternity I wish for him. I still cry out for him, though, a cry that comes from deep within, without my volition. I don't know whether to be glad or sad that he never responds.

Ever since Jeff died, I've gotten in the bad habit of playing computer games—Spider Solitaire, Mahjong Titans, Freecell. It's almost pathological the way I need them to work out. I keep redoing them until I win. In this one way, I can rework the past to make it come out right, and it satisfies something in me. I wish we could do the same thing with life. But maybe we do? Somehow keep reworking the same life until it comes out right? Sounds depressing.

Guess I'll just keep chugging away at this life. Maybe it will turn out right in the end.

Day 81, **Dear Jeff,**

I'm still having a hard time getting along without you. As hard as last year was getting along with you, this is a thousand times worse. I still regret that I wasn't more patient with you, but I was truly bewildered (and irritated) by some of your eccentric behavior. I had no way of knowing you had cancer and that it had spread to your brain.

I haven't yet segued into thinking this is my life. It still seems to be our life, and our separation temporary. When it hits me that I'm never going home to you, it hurts unbearably. You'd think by now the truth would have sunk in for good, but maybe I don't want it to. The truth is too bleak.

I never did find out the why of us. We got so caught up in daily life that our meeting, our connection seemed less mystical than practical, but something was going on beneath surface consciousness. You once told me that at the end of one July you were lonely and wished you had someone in your life. A week later, I stopped by your store for the first time. We always joked that you conjured me up. But perhaps it was no joke. I'm grateful you shared so much of yourself with me, grateful we had the adventures we did, grateful we had so much time together. Thank you for sharing your life with me.

Adios, compadre. I love you.

Day 82, Blog Post, **The Long and Winding Road of Grief**
The problem with grief (not counting the primary problem of having lost a loved one) is that so many emotions attack you all at once that you feel you can never get a grip. And then, for no fathomable reason, you hit an emotional trough where you feel nothing, and you begin to think that you can handle your grief, and then . . . pow! Out of nowhere, it returns and slams you in the gut.

I was never a wildly emotional person, but now I am buffeted by more different emotions in a single day than I used to experience in a month. The emotions are not all negative, either. This morning, I woke up feeling a tingle of excitement—I'd planned to go on a long ramble, camera in hand, and for the first time in months, perhaps years, I felt alive. I've always taken long walks, but for the past couple of decades I've lived on a .3-mile lane between a dead end and a busy highway, so I used to walk up and down the lane, always looking for anything different to make the trek interesting. Now, I don't have to look for those differences—I have a brand new world beneath my feet, before my eyes, and something in me is responding.

But still, side-by-side with my new awakening, is the sorrow that my mate is no longer with me. About fifteen minutes before I returned from my walk today, the thought that he was not waiting for me at the end doubled me over with pain. After such a bout, when the immediacy of the pain passes, when the tears finally dissipate, I'm left with the inexplicable feeling that he is away, perhaps getting well, and one of these days he will be calling, telling me I can come home. But he won't be calling. And I won't be going home.

And so I continue walking the long and winding road of grief.

Day 83, **Grief Journal**

I'm not doing much. Just drifting. Getting through the days. Pretending to be real. I hope the rest of my life isn't going to be just marking time like this. It sounds . . . feeble. Mostly I'm babying myself, as if I'm recovering from a long illness. And I am—a soul sickness.

I spend hours every day wandering in the desert. I'm as restless as Jeff was at the end, and walking seems to be the only thing that keeps me pacified. The past couple of weeks have felt like a perfect summer from childhood that was always warm and sunny, at least in memory. It's been hot here, of course, and windy, but I've been roaming like a child newly freed from restrictions.

I hope I am going somewhere. I hope I'm growing, developing, doing something besides stagnating, which is how I feel.

Day 86, Blog Post, **Twelve Lonely Weeks**

It's been twelve weeks since my life mate died—twelve lonely weeks that I've spent wishing he were here, wishing that we had our life back, wishing that he hadn't been sick so much.

I'm beginning to understand, though, that to wish things were different is to negate the wisdom, courage, and determination with which he faced his life and death. Until the very end when he was imprisoned in bed by drugs (They did not know how else to handle his terminal restlessness—the restlessness that some people experience near the end—so they tranquilized him into a coma.), he was determined to live his life to the fullest he could. He was so weak, so befuddled by the drugs and the metastases in his brain that he could not do much, yet his courage and determination were as strong as ever. Sick of being in bed, sick of being sick, he set up an office in the living room and set to work planning his schedule. That was the last night he was awake. He lived through five more nights and days, but he was not conscious. Or at least I hope he wasn't. He would have hated being a helpless invalid, so it's a good thing he only had to endure five such days.

I really was glad—or perhaps relieved is a better word – when he died. He'd suffered so much and that determination of his not to waste a single moment of his life, not to give in to the disease, kept him going long after he was ready to die. Later, as the reality of the situation hit me, as grief devastated me, I began to wish things had been different.

He'd been told he had three to six months to live, but he only had three weeks. I've been wishing we had those months—but even if I had a choice, there is no way I could justify putting him through that extra pain so I could have him in my life a little longer.

And yet . . . and yet. I still wish things had been different. I wish he'd had a long, healthy, happy life. I wish we still had "our" life.

I wish I could hug him one more time.

I wish . . .

Day 87, **Dear Jeff,**

I always thought your perpetual calendar was a bit silly—if a day goes by and you forget to change the date, how would you know what date it was? Still, I've been doing it—changing the date every morning. It's a brief memorial to you. I don't need to write you anymore, not since I've taken to talking to you as part of that morning ritual (mourning ritual?), but I still like writing to you. Makes me feel connected to you.

I'm having a hard time thinking only of me. I look for interesting news items to tell you. When I go to the grocery store, I look for foods to tempt your appetite. Life-long habits of caring don't die just because the loved one did.

I don't feel changed, but shouldn't I? At the very least, shouldn't I feel lighter, happier, relieved that your illness is no longer burdening my life? I didn't feel burdened, though, not until that last year when you seemed such a stranger. I know you were a stranger even to yourself, and no wonder with all that cancer in your brain.

The more I think about that year, the more I admire you. Despite horrendous exhaustion and pain, you did what you had to do to survive another day, to accomplish something. You had such courage.

Adios, compadre. I love you. I miss you.

Day 88, **Grief Journal**

I'm getting organized somewhat, setting up my "office," finding places to put the things I brought with me, but am far from completing the task. There is no "done" in my life, just "doing." No reason to finish anything.

It will be good when I know where everything is, though. For some reason, every time I can't find something, it sets off a storm of grief. Tears galore.

Although I got rid of so many of Jeff's things, I hesitate to get rid of others, such as his music tapes. Part of me thinks he'll need them, but if he wants to listen to music, he can pluck it out of the air. Don't radio waves travel forever? Maybe it's the same with the songs he once listened to.

I try to believe that he isn't truly gone, but it isn't a thought I can hold on to. I know something survives—the energy?—but try as I might, I can't believe we will meet again, or if we do, that we will recognize each other. Yet there is something beyond us (within us?), because where did that inner wail come from when I met him? I can still hear it: *but I don't even like men with blond hair and brown eyes.* Not exactly love at first sight. More like recognition. But recognition of what?

Day 89, **Dear Jeff,**

I'm spending a lot of time with you lately—talking to you, writing to you, watching movies with you. And yet, in truth, I am spending no time with you, just with my memories of you and the box of your pulverized bone. I am afraid I'm moving beyond you too quickly, that soon—way before I'm ready—I'll be so far from "us" and "our" life that you will no longer be part of "my" life. I know you're not part of it anymore since you are no more, but I am not ready to face that. Don't know if I ever will be able to.

How could thirty-four years have evaporated? I try to grasp our years together, but they are forever out of reach. As are you. I know I have to go on alone, to figure out a way to live, to survive, to be, but not just yet. Stay with me a while longer. Please?

Watching your movies helps. I feel as if we are watching them together, even though our togetherness is removed in time. But if there is no time, as some scientists say, then your watching the movie a year ago and my watching today could be construed as our watching the movie together.

Let me know if there's anything in particular you'd like to watch. Adios, compadre. I love you.

Day 92, **Dear Jeff,**

Can you see me crying? I've had good days—or rather, days that haven't been as bad as others—but today I'm in agony. Why did you leave me? Even though it wasn't your fault, I still feel as if you abandoned me. I dread the day it hits me deep down in my soul that you are dead, that I will never be going home to you, that I will never see you again.

I've been keeping myself busy so that I don't cry as much anymore, at least not for hours on end as I used to. Grief surges several times a day, but generally doesn't last long. I think it's because I'm not depressed, which, oddly makes

63

things worse. When depression is the bedrock of grief, tears go on and on and then slowly peter out. But for me, grief comes and goes in an instant. I can be fine, and then all of a sudden be awash in tears, and just as suddenly return to normal—my new normal, that is.

Today is different, though. It's Saturday, thirteen weeks since your death, and tomorrow it will be three months. I can't stop crying. My one comfort is that you are no longer suffering.

I will get through this somehow, I promise.

Day 93, Blog Post, **I Am a Three-Month Grief Survivor**

Grief plays tricks with time. The past three months have passed in the blink of an eye, and they have lasted forever. I never thought I'd last three weeks let alone three months—at times the pain was so unbearable I wanted to scream. So I did.

Yet here I am, a thousand miles from where I started, and generally I'm doing okay. Grief grabs me a couple of times a day, but doesn't hang around long, mostly because I take long walks and look at life through the lens of a camera. I find solace there, and peace.

This morning, however, I woke in tears because of this new milestone—three months since his death. I needed to scream, to be alone with my pain, so I headed out for a walk. Wandered in the desert. Cried in the wilderness. And screamed. Haven't had to do that for a while—I've been keeping myself too busy to feel much, so it was good, in a strange and agonizing sort of way, to reconnect with my grief.

I'm still going to a grief support group. It does help to be around people who understand this journey, to hear how others are handling their loss. (Loss. What an odd way to describe death, as if the person is simply misplaced, like a ring, and will soon be found.) Each week there is a special focus of attention, a lesson. The lesson for the grief support group last week was about finding a sense of purpose and accepting that for now we are where we must be.

I'm not sure that I am where I need to be, either mentally or geographically, but I am trying to trust in the rightness of my path, and that I will know what to do when the next step comes. What bothers me is that by trusting in the rightness of the path, both mine and my soul mate's, it means that it was right for him to be sick and die, and that I cannot accept. But maybe it's not up to me to accept the rightness of his path, only the rightness of mine.

As for change? If I were writing a novel about a character who has gone through what I have these past months—first the diagnosis of his illness, then his too quick death, then sorting through the accumulation of decades, and moving from the house where we spent the past twenty years—she would have grown stronger perhaps, or wiser, and changed in some fundamental way, but I don't feel any different. I'm still the same person, though my situation is completely different than it was six months ago.

But perhaps it's too soon for any change to appear. In the world of grief, I am still a toddler.

Fourth Month

Day 99, **Dear Jeff,**

Another day gone. I'm trying to mark the days, to make them . . . not memorable. Important, maybe? I've told you I don't care whether I live or die, and it's true, but I am still alive, so I might as well live the best I can. I'm trying to capture the days and not let them slip through my fingers, even if it's only by appreciating a flower or noting the temperature of the air.

Do you see the smudges on this page? Tears. It's Saturday, and I always cry on Saturday now. Fourteen weeks since you've been gone. I miss you. I miss "us." Now there is just me. I'm getting used to it, but I still wish I could talk with you about your being gone.

I hope you're dealing with this better than I am, Jeff.

Day 100, **Grief Journal**

I hate that Jeff is gone. I DO NOT want to do this. I'm doing okay, I guess, I just don't want to have to do what it takes to survive this grief. It's too damn hard. I have no energy, no ideas, no belief that anything good will happen.

And yet, I would hate to think I could just glide into the future without a thought for Jeff and the life we shared. My grief matters because he mattered.

Day 101, **Dear Jeff,**

I called for you when I was out walking in the desert today, but you didn't answer. Well, of course you didn't answer—you're dead.

I kept walking, following the winding road wherever it took me. No view on the road was different from another. The road didn't lead to any particular place. The point was just to go. To see. And so it is with my life right now. I have no real reason to do anything. There is no meaning in my life, no reason to live except for curiosity (such an active word to describe the passivity of my interest). I had no idea you would leave such a void in my life. Had no idea that being with you diminished the meaninglessness I once struggled with. Had no idea your absence would rekindle that meaninglessness. Had no idea how hard it would be to continue without you.

We were together for more than three decades, but I can't remember a lot of it. Is it because of the persistent shock of your dying? I remember most clearly the end times—pacing hand-in-hand with you, your cheery "adios, compadre," your gentle, almost playful last kiss. Mixed in with all this is my final sight of your gaunt face and a thousand visions of your being sick. Why can't I remember many robust times?

I do remember our meeting, the first time our fingers touched, the wonder of loving you, but so many details are lost in the entirety of our lives. Maybe I don't need to remember the details or to picture your face. You're in the very fiber of my being.

Your being gone has left an immense hole and one heck of a lot of tears. I still cry several times a day. I'm still hugging your ashes, for cripes sake. I can't get it through my skull that you're gone and I'll never see you again.

Adios, compadre. Take care of yourself.

Day 102, Blog Post, **Grief Has It's Own Logic**

Grief is not a gentle slope. It does not start at the top (or the bottom) and gradually diminish. It comes in peaks and valleys. And sometimes it comes when one least expects it. I was okay for a couple of days, successfully bypassing the minefields of memory—I've learned what of our things bring me comfort and what brings me pain—but then yesterday the grief spiked, and it's as it was in the beginning.

It was such a silly thing that set off this new spate of grief. I washed our comforters, and as I was folding them and putting them in the zipper bags they came in, I thought how nice and fresh they will be when my life mate and I get back together. Then it struck me—again—that he is gone. We're not taking separate vacations, nor I am waiting for him to come home from the hospital, but apparently, somewhere in the back of my mind, that is what I believe.

One of my blog readers recommended Joan Didion's book *The Year of Magical Thinking*, which was written the year after Joan's husband died. My blog reader hoped the book would bring me the comfort that it brought her. And it did bring me the comfort of knowing that this illogical thinking, this magical thinking, is part of the grief process. Although Joan had no trouble getting rid of her husband's clothes, she could not get rid of his shoes because he might need them. Although I got rid of my mate's car (I donated it to hospice, thinking that since I took him there, that is where his car should go.), I could not get rid of his extra set of keys because he might need them. I got rid of a brand new television but could not get rid of a pencil stub because the stub seemed so much like him—he used up everything, wasted nothing. I could not get rid of his eyeglasses, because how will he see without them?

I am not a bubbly, rose-colored glasses sort of person, but I always managed to find an "at least" in every situation, an "upside." Until now. This is one time when there is no at least. (Yes, I know at least he is no longer suffering, but he shouldn't have had to suffer in the first place.) There is no upside. I know I will eventually find my way to a new life, perhaps even happiness, but it does not change the fact that he is dead.

Every day I feel his absence. Every day, in some way, I try to rework the events of the past few months so that he really will return to me. But that is not going to happen in this lifetime. And so I trudge the hills of grief, and treasure the moments of comfort I find.

Day 104, Blog Post, **Rewinding My Life**
I ended my last blog post with: *And so I trudge the hills of grief, and treasure the moments of comfort I find.* I meant it both figuratively and literally—I spend a couple of hours most days wandering in the desert hills near where I am staying.

I feel at times as if I am rewinding my life, our life. When the man I was to spend more than three decades with first came into my life, it was such an awesome change, that I felt restless. I would walk for hours trying to get used to this new vision (or version) of me. I wrote. And I read copiously. Now that he has left my life, it's such a traumatic change that I feel restless. I walk for hours trying to get used to this new vision/version of me. Instead of walking through the tree-shaded parks and parkways of Denver, however, I tramp through the desert a thousand miles from where I started.

Instead of poetry, I write prose. And I read copiously. These are the bookends of our shared life.

During the years of his illness, when I tried to imagine how it would be to live alone again after his death, I never imagined, never could imagine, the sheer void of his absence and with it, the absence of meaning.

Before I met him, I used to wonder about the meaning of life. Now, once again, I am wondering about the meaning of life. I hadn't realized until after he was gone that during all those years we were together, I didn't worry about meaning.

We were together. That was all that mattered. Now that I am alone once more, the void of meaningless haunts me. Where am I going? And why?

I did have a bit of revelation out in the desert the other day. Instead of a stroke of clarity, I might have had heat stroke, but the end result is still the same. I walked for hours along a path because I was curious where it went, curious to see what was around the next bend, and it occurred to me that this experience could be a metaphor for my life. Perhaps finding meaning isn't important. Perhaps it's enough simply to follow the days and see where they lead.

Day 107, Blog Post, **Nor All Your Tears**

> The Moving Finger writes, and having writ,
> Moves on: nor all your Piety nor Wit
>   Shall lure it back to cancel half a line,
> Nor all your tears wash out a Word of it.

When I started writing, I often thought of the above quatrain from the "Rubaiyat of Omar Kayyam." It made me smile to reflect that this warning about the moving finger does not hold true when it comes to writing. We writers can—and should—rewrite and rewrite until the story turns out exactly the way we want it to turn out.

When it comes to real life and especially death, however, there is no rewriting. If the story does not turn out the way we want, too bad. And tears, as I now know from experience, will not wash away a single moment of what has already happened.

No matter how much I cry, my mate is still dead.

I worry sometimes about talking so much about my crying for him (and for me). Perhaps people will see me as weak since people often equate tears with spinelessness and immaturity. There is certainly something babyish about crying for that which one cannot have, for wailing against that which one cannot change. Sometimes I think I should be braver about this traumatic turn my life has taken, or more stoic. Still, tears are the only way I have of momentarily relieving the terrible ache of his absence. And this reason for tears is true not only for me.

I met a woman who cannot cry over the death of her husband, though she wants to. People have suggested that she cut onions to stimulate tears, but research shows that tears released by such irritations are different from those released because of emotion. Dr. William Frey, a biochemist and director of the Dry Eye and Tear Research Center in Minneapolis, says that people "may be removing, in their tears, chemicals that build up during emotional stress." So crying is not a sign of weakness. Abstaining from crying is not a sign of bravery.

Tears are simply that—tears—though I wish with all my heart they were more, that they had the power to wash away the past and bring my mate back to me, healthy and happy.

Day 108, Grief Journal

I'm getting used to my tears, but I am not getting used to Jeff being gone. I hate the finality of death. Why can't I see him again? Why can't I talk with him? It doesn't seem as if that's too much to ask. I'm not sure what I'd say if I did see him. I do know I'd hold him fast.

I wish we could have hugged more that last year, but every touch brought him pain. Just another thing to grieve.

I truly do not understand grief. I seem to get sadder all the time. Perhaps I am more aware of my sadness? Less stunned by his death? I'm tired of Jeff being dead. That's all there is to it. I miss him more than I ever imagined.

Day 110, Blog Post: Grief's Milestones

The first year of grieving is difficult, not just because the wounds to the heart and mind are so raw and the void where the loved one resided so dark, but because it is a year of firsts. And each of these firsts comes with a renewal of pain.

We—my life mate and I—did not celebrate our birthdays. We merely recognized them as a tally mark for another year gone by. Because of this, I had not expected to feel any

71

deeper sadness today—his birthday—than I felt yesterday or the day before, but grief knows no logic. It doesn't matter that we never celebrated his birthday—that was his choice. But that he is not here to make that choice does matter, and so I'm dealing with an upsurge of grief. We will no longer be marking his years. He will never grow older. Perhaps next year I will be able to let the day pass without making a big deal of it, but today is a first. One of grief's milestones. His first birthday after death.

I know these days of refreshed pain are important. Too often I keep myself busy to minimize the pain, and there is no effective way to get around true grieving but to feel the pain and go through it. Or so I've been told. Reconnecting with the pain is also a way of reconnecting to him. The faster I go through the grief process, the further I get from him. The *farther* I get from him.

The earth hurtles around the sun at 67,000 mph. The sun hurtles around the galaxy at 140 miles per second. The entire universe is also moving and expanding, so today we are a very long way from where we were when he died. (Considering only the speed of the earth, he died 165,356,000 miles ago.)

And, considering only the surface distance, I am almost 1000 miles from where we lived. We planted trees and bushes around the house to keep it cool and to give us privacy, and that green world seems a million miles from the desert where I am staying now.

So, today I am celebrating his birthday, if only with my grief, because it helps me bridge the distance.

Day 112, **Grief Journal,**

I'm going through a numb phase right now. I only cried briefly yesterday. That came after I finished watching the Paul Hogan/Michael Caton movie Jeff taped—*Strange Bedfellows*—and I realized I'd never watch movies with him again.

Cry, not cry. Feel, not feel. It's all the same. Just different aspects of grief. One thing they're right about. This is

WORK! I'm tired, have little energy, don't seem to be able to think or to do anything but the most basic chores. And I can't make myself believe anything is important. I'm still waiting to get a grip on my grief. Still feeling as if I'm in a transitional stage, waiting for my life to start.

Except that I had a life. *We* had a life.

People talk about "healing" when it comes to surviving a death, and it's as good a term as any. It does seem as if the wound where Jeff was amputated from me is still bloody and gaping, though it is "healing" somewhat. It's not as constantly raw as it was at first.

I always felt scattered when we were apart, worried about something happening to one of us when the other wasn't there. Well, something did happen. And I was there. Now it's just me. Wherever I am, there I am, but I still feel scattered. Fragmented. As if parts of me are strewn all over the universe. There's no reason to worry about him, but I still do.

Day 115, **Dear Jeff,**

Did you use the phrase okie-doke one night at the end when you were saying all those jaunty things like "adios, compadre"? You must have. Every time I see or hear the expression, I start crying. Good thing it's not in common usage any more.

I am hurtling away from you at incredible speeds. Maybe I'll come full circle and meet with you again when my end arrives? I wish I believed that, but it makes no sense. How do sparks of energy have cognizance, character, memory? How would we know each other? At least I would no longer have to deal with your absence since I'd be absent too.

You came into my life so rapidly. One day you weren't there, and the next you were. You went out the same way. One day you were there, the next you weren't.

Yesterday someone told me that life on earth was an illusion and so you still existed. But if life is an illusion, why couldn't it be a happy figment? A joyful one? What's the point of pain? Of loss? Of suffering?

You've been gone one-hundred and fifteen days, and I still can't make sense of it.

Adios, compadre. I hope you, at least, are at peace.

Day 123, Blog Post, **I Am a Four-Month Grief Survivor**

People who have not suffered a devastating loss don't understand grief, and those who have suffered such a loss often cannot describe what they are going through. No wonder few writers are able to accurately portray a grieving person.

I read a novel the other day about a woman who lost her husband, and the only acknowledgment of her grief was a single sentence: *She went through all five of the Kübler-Ross stages of grief.* I wish grief were that simple, that clinical, but grief is one of the most complicated—and agonizing—states a person will ever suffer. There are not just five stages of grief, or even seven. There seems to be an infinite shading of emotions in the process we call grief, and Kübler-Ross's stages form the merest scaffolding.

We bereft do feel shock, denial, anger, guilt, sadness, depression, and perhaps acceptance. (I say perhaps because I can't vouch for acceptance since I have not yet reached such a stage. In fact, I fight it—what right do I have to say it's acceptable for my life mate to have died?) We also feel anxiety, frustration, loneliness, confusion, despair, helplessness, panic, questioning (both as a need to know why and as a cry of pain), loss or gain of faith, loss of identity, loss of self-esteem, identifying with the deceased (taking on their characteristics or wearing their clothes), resentment, bitterness, isolation, inability to focus, suspended animation, waiting for we know not what, envy of those who are still coupled or who have yet to suffer a loss. And we suffer myriad physical symptoms such as queasiness, dizziness, sleep problems (too much or too little), eating problems (too much or too little), bone-deep pain, inability at times to breath or swallow, exhaustion, lack of energy, restlessness, and seemingly endless bouts of tears.

Even worse, we do not move through these stages one at

a time as if it were a checklist, but we experience several emotions and ailments at once. Worst of all, we visit each of these states again and again. I suppose there is an end to this spiral of grief, but I am so far from seeing the closing stages that I have to put my head down and endure however I can.

If there were a market for tears, I would be a very rich woman.

Every time I think I'm getting on solid footing, something happens to slam me back into the black hole of grief. The hardest times to get through are the day of the week he died (Saturday) and the day of the month (the 27th). Sometimes unexpectedly coming across a note in his handwriting reminds me of all I am missing. Other times such a find makes me feel close to him. There is no logic to grief. It has its own timetable, its own method, and whenever I think I understand the process, grief changes its tactics.

I am a private person (at least I was until grief turned my life inside out) and not a joiner. But after he died, I was in such unbearable pain I didn't know what to do, so I went to a bereavement group sponsored by hospice. When I relocated, I started in with a new group. It's good to be with people who understand, who have suffered what I am suffering. It's good to know that one can survive. It's good to see a bit of life growing in the cracks of grief.

You'd think that after all this, I would know what to say to someone who has suffered a loss similar to mine, but I am as tongue-tied as the uninitiated. A friend recently lost her mate of two decades, and all I had to offer her were my tears.

So much sadness. So much anguish. I still don't know how any of us get through this, but we do.

Fifth Month

Day 131, Blog Post, **Grief is Not a Medical Disorder**

According to the new *Diagnostic and Statistical Manual of Mental Disorders* released by the American Psychiatric Association, grief is considered a medical disorder, and should be treated as major depression. There used to be a bereavement exclusion in the description of major depression, but they have taken that away, and now more than a few days of pain is considered a crisis. There can be "a few days of acute upset and then a much longer period of the longing, the tearfulness. But typically sleep, appetite, energy, concentration come back to normal more quickly than that."

In whose world is grieving a medical condition that needs to be treated? Not my world. In my world, grief is one of the bookends of a relationship. Love. Grief. If grief is a medical condition, then watch out. One day love is going to be considered a treatable disease.

Perhaps emotional pain is not necessary. Perhaps people can survive quite nicely without going through the pain of grief—perhaps avoiding grief won't cause the future problems people say it will—but the truth is, grief is a life experience, an incredibly deep and painful and raw experience that changes the way you think about yourself and the world. Grief helps you process the amputation of having a child or a mate torn from your life, let's you experience the loss in a visceral way, makes it real. In past eras, grief was acceptable, in fact, was even encouraged. In today's world, grief needs to be hidden so that it doesn't offend people's sensibilities, so that it doesn't bring the specter of bad luck into people's lives. Drugs can hide your grief, of course, but that's all it can do.

I didn't grieve excessively when my mother or my brother died, but when my mate died? I was devastated. (Still am, but at the moment I am going through a hiatus, a time of peace.) It wasn't only the death of him. It was the death of our future, our dreams, our hopes, our lifestyle, our shared life, our private jokes. It was the death of my companion, my love, my friend, my confidante, my fellow traveler on life's journey. No drug is going to make any of those deaths acceptable.

"He" died. "We" died. But "I" didn't. Grief made me realize that. Surviving grief has taught me that I can survive anything. No drug could ever give me that.

I know a woman who mourned the loss of her mother for two years. Actually, she wasn't mourning the loss of the mother so much as the loss of the emotional support and attachment the mother never gave her and now never would. She emerged from this period a strong, vital, wise woman. No drug could ever give her that.

In a strange way, grief is a gift. Easy? No. Painful? Yes. But . . . If you let yourself feel it, let it become a part of you, it will take you where you need to go. And no drug can ever give you that.

Day 135, Blog Post, **One Woman's Grief**

The American Psychiatric Association has labeled grief that lasts more than a few weeks a mental disorder. I wrote about this in my last blog post, "Grief Is Not a Medical Disorder," but I can't stop thinking about it. The problem with grief is not the pain, though sometimes the agony is so unbearable it takes one's breath away, but the reason for the pain: a very dear person, a part of your life, is gone and will never return. When one is depressed for no reason, then perhaps the misery can be classified as a mental disorder. But if there is a reason for the pain, if there is a direct cause for the depression, then it is not a disorder. It is life.

Grief varies, of course. Everyone grieves in a different way, and everyone feels each subsequent death in a different way. The loss of an aged aunt you barely knew is different from the loss of a beloved mate. In the first case, prolonged grief could be a sign of depression, but in the second case, prolonged grief is a way of coping.

When I lost my mate, I was in such pain I thought my

heart would burst. I couldn't breath, couldn't focus, couldn't see how I could ever get through the day let alone the rest of my life. I was also still in shock from witnessing his horrific death.

I did get through those first days, though how I don't know—the pain escalated by the minute. Then I found out about a local bereavement support group. I am a private person, one who keeps her emotions to herself, but I went to the group meeting anyway hoping someone could tell me how to deal with the pain. No one could, of course, but I did meet people who had survived a similar loss, and that taught me survival was possible. One of the problems with grief is how it isolates you, and the group made me feel less isolated. And that was a comfort.

I had no intention of writing much about grief on this blog. I posted a few articles mentioning my pain, and found that not only did the articles help me, they gave comfort and support to others who were going through the same thing. So I continue to write about grief. Perhaps someday the private me will look around and be aghast at all I have made public, but for now, it's my way of coping.

The point of this bloggery is that the pain of grief made me reach out and let others into my world. If I had been treated for depression during this time, I wouldn't have connected with others. I would have remained isolated, and the effects of intense grief would have lasted much longer than they did. Everyone has the right to grieve the way they want, of course, but feeling the pain was the only way I could do it, both for me and for my mate. He deserved to have someone grieve that he died, to have someone feel the imbalance of the world without him in it. And that is not a mental disorder.

Day 142, Blog Post, **Sorry For Your Loss**

Cops, social workers, therapists, just about anyone who deals with death in any capacity, learn to give an automatic, "I'm sorry for your loss," to the bereaved. At first, this condolence by rote bothered me. It came across as insensitive and . . . well, automatic. Besides, it seemed to reduce the death of my mate to the level of a lost sock. I don't mind as much now. Even though I have been born into the world of grief, I still don't know what to say to someone who is grieving. Besides, grief *is* about loss, and not just the primary loss of a loved one, but also multiple secondary losses.

In my case, when I lost my life mate, I lost my home (my mate was my home even more than the house we lived in, but I lost that too when I had to move away). I lost the future we planned. I lost the hopes we had. I lost my best friend. I lost my partner. I lost my lifestyle. I lost the one person who knew everything about me and liked me anyway. I lost the person I could depend on to be there when I needed him. And most of all, I lost myself.

It's not so much that I saw myself as an adjunct to him, or that my identity depended on him, but he was the focus of my life for more than three decades. By his very being, he gave my life meaning. Before we met, I always wondered about the meaning of life. I wanted to live a significant life, to make sure my life meant something. After we met, I didn't worry about such things—at least, not much. It was important that we were together, that we faced the world together. Only after his death did I realize how much "togetherness" mattered to me. And the loss of that togetherness is something to mourn.

Now that I am alone, I have to find meaning in "aloneness," to find significance in that aloneness. And I don't know if I can. I feel fractured, as if bits of me are scattered all over the universe, and I haven't a clue how to put myself together again. Oddly enough, I had no real interest in spending my years with anyone until he entered my life. And now I am back where I started. Sort of.

I feel a bit foolish (and self-pitying) at times for all the tears I shed. I always thought I was more stoic than this, able to take life's big dramas in stride. Yet the deletion of him from the earth is impossible for me to fathom. It affects every single aspect of my life. I haven't found the bedrock of my new life—the thing, the idea, the place, whatever that bedrock might be—that gives me a firm footing and allows me to get on with my life. He's been gone for twenty weeks (is that a lot or a little? I no longer have any sense of time) and everything is still resettling. If I get a grip on one facet of my loss, another secondary loss rises to the surface. And so his absence (and my loss) becomes more profound as time passes.

I've been trying to write again, and even in such an exercise that epitomizes aloneness, I feel his absence. I used to read what I wrote to him. He didn't always have a suggestion or a comment, but sometimes he'd get a little smile on his face when I hit the scene just right. And that smile is just one more loss for which I am sorry.

Day 146, Blog Post, **In Grief, There Will Not Be Closure**

In our society, for whatever reason—perhaps because of the manic need to be positive, because of a short attention span, because of ignorance of what grief entails—after four to six months, most people seem to lose patience with outward shows of grief from the bereft. No wonder depression peaks six months after the death of a loved one—grievers are left alone to suffer in silence when they most need comfort.

I am still a long way from that six-month period, but already I sense impatience from others whenever my grief bleeds over into my real life, though my grief doesn't often show. I can carry on a conversation, smile and laugh at appropriate times, concede that yes, I am finding closure.

I don't know who wrote this, but it reinforces what we grievers have come to understand:

At some point we begin to find the road to life again and begin to retain a productive life. This is not closure. Closure is a term that was invented to make other people feel better. We will not experience closure and shouldn't. We will miss our loved one and will never forget. As time goes by it gets easier and we learn to cope with the necessary changes, but there will not be closure.

Sometimes there is closure, especially if the deceased did not play a major role in our lives, but after any significant loss, we muddle along as best as we can with a big hole in our heart. It might scab over. We might learn to love again. But there will not be closure.

Very few people manage to live their entire life without a major loss, but still grief makes people uncomfortable. Almost no one knows what to say to the bereft, which adds an interesting bit of irony to grief. It is the bereft who must be sensitive to the needs of would-be comforters, to be understanding when confronted with insensitivity, to bring comfort to the uncomfortable. We've all encountered insensitive remarks (like "how could he have allowed himself to get cancer?") yet we take the comments in the spirit we hope they were given.

Even though I have to let others feel better by thinking I'm finding closure, it's nice to be able to tell the truth here in this blog: I am still grieving. And there will not be closure.

Day 154, Blog Post, **I Am a Five-Month Grief Survivor**

Five months ago, my life mate died . . . and I am surviving. I had not expected to grieve much—he had suffered a long time, and his death was hard-won—but still, those first endless weeks were difficult. The delineation between "us together" and "me alone" was so abrupt, so stark, so uncompromising that I had a hard time fathoming it. I finally went to a grief support group to find out how one survives such pain. I never did find out, but I discovered that one can survive the trauma, which helped, as did talking about my experience and listening to what others had to say. Grief is so isolating that it's nice not to feel alone.

What helped most of all, though, was simply living. During the past five months, I have read dozens of books, walked hundreds of miles, written thousands of words, taken I-don't-know-how-many photos, met many people both online and offline. All of those experiences have helped create memories, memories of a life without him, and those

81

memories have softened the threshold between "us together" and "me alone." I still have times of great sadness, still have that falling-elevator feeling when I remember I will never see him again, still miss him (probably always will), but for the most part I am doing okay.

I've abandoned my mental crutches—I no longer write a letter to him every day, don't talk to him very often, don't feel a need to scream. I am thinking more of the future, which signifies hope and getting on with my life, but such thoughts also bring moments of panic when I think of having to grow old alone. Mostly, I try to live in the moment and take each day as it comes.

One big trauma this past month was when I finally accepted in my depths that I will never see him again in this life. I knew that from the beginning, of course, but knowing it, feeling it, and accepting it are completely different things. People talk about acceptance as if it's a peaceful thing, yet at the time, it felt as if I were losing him all over again. But that passed as everything does.

One big advancement this past month happened just this morning—for the first time since his death, I smiled when I thought of him. He would be pleased—he'd have hated being the cause of so much pain.

He was a good man. I'm glad he shared his life with me.

Sixth Month

Day 158, Blog Post, **Sucker-Punched by Grief**

After the first excruciating months, dealing with a major loss is like being in the ring with an ever-weakening opponent. The feeble jabs inflict little pain, and you start feeling as if you can go the distance. Gradually, as the blows come further and further apart, you let down your guard. You even welcome the blows that do land, because they remind you why you are fighting. Then . . .

Wham!

Out of nowhere comes the knockout punch.

My knockout punch came after a restless night. I finally fell asleep in the early morning hours, and I dreamt.

I dreamed that my life mate was dead, but I woke to find him alive and getting well. It was wonderful seeing him doing so much better, and a quiet joy seeped over me.

I started to wake. In the seconds before full consciousness hit, I continued to feel the joy of knowing he still lived. And then . . .

Wham!

The truth hit me. I couldn't breathe, couldn't move. Then, like an aftershock, came the raw pain, the heartbreak of losing him . . . again.

I'd only dreamt about him once before, and that was at the beginning when my defenses were still in place. In that first dream, I told him I thought he'd died, but deep down I knew the truth, and there was no shock when I awoke, just a feeling of gladness that I got to see him once more. But this time, I had let down my guard. I'd even felt a bit smug that I was getting a grip on my grief so early in the process, and so the dream caught me unaware. In the depths of my being, I believed that he hadn't died.

I cried on and off for two or three days (I lost count; grief tends to override time) but now I've regained my equilibrium—at least until the next time.

A friend who counsels the bereft told me, "In my experience with grief, a healthy person, such as yourself, is going to grieve in a gradually diminishing way for two years."

Two years??!!

If so, I have a very long way to go. I'd planned to stop blogging about grief. I don't want people to think I am eliciting sympathy, nor do I want to seem pathetic, grieving long after the non-bereft think I should be done with it. But if I'm going to have bouts of pain for many months to come, I might as well share them and let others take whatever comfort they can from my learning experiences.

This episode with the dream taught me to be patient with myself. I've been thinking that I'm mostly healed, and I've been feeling like a slacker, just taking life a moment at a time, not doing anything to prepare for the rest of my life, not doing much of anything but reading, walking, writing a little (a very little), taking photographs, and going through my mate's collection of movies. Now that I know the power of the sucker punch, and how easily it can gain the upper hand, I understand this simple life is all I can expect of me right now. And perhaps that's the way it's supposed to be.

Day 159, **Dear Jeff,**

I can't get that dream out of my mind. I can still feel the tension of missing you seep away when I thought your death had been a dream, and the utter pain of waking up to the truth.

There is such a hole in me, such an inability to grasp the meaning of your absence, that I am totally lost and bewildered. I want—*need*—something I can never have. It's like a hunger—a skin hunger, a mind hunger. I cannot comprehend what your death means except that I'm left alone to find my own way.

Damn it! I know we're not the only people this ever happened to—I've heard so many sad tales these past months—but it happened to *us*.

You worked so hard to be healthy, you deserved to be

healthy. You worked so hard to be strong, you deserved to be strong. Even with all the reality we had to face, I believed somewhere, somehow it would all work out for you, for me, for us. I know you were impatient with that belief—you wanted me to face the truth and to understand what was going to happen, but I was naïve in so many ways. I had no idea what death meant—the total end, the line that can never be recrossed, the sheer absence of the dead one. I still don't know what it means, still can't comprehend your goneness.

Does anything happen by our choice? In small matters, yes. But in big ones? I don't see it. I look back at the past few years, trying to figure out what we could have done differently so that everything would have worked out for us, but all our efforts seemed to have led inexorably to your end.

What's the point of it all? Why do we cling so much to life? In the eternal scheme of things, does it matter how long or short a life is? Does it matter that you only had sixty-three years? It sure matters to me! I want you in my life. I want you to have a life.

I read an article in the paper today that talked about stream-of-consciousness being the brain's default mode. The journalist said that in depression, the default mode network appears to be overactive, that a depressive brain shows a pattern of balky transitions from introspective thought to work that requires conscious effort, and it frequently slips into the default mode during cognitive tasks. A depressive brain also shows especially weak links between the default mode network and a region of the brain involved in motivation and reward-seeking behavior.

Is this why I so seldom see the point in anything, why it's hard to find a reason to do things? Is this why stream-of-consciousness writing is easy for me, but fiction is so difficult?

I'm surprised I'm not severely depressed with your being gone. I'm sad and in pain, but not in the black hole of despair. I can cry and be sad, but when the episode passes, I'll be fine. Or I can be fine until something tilts me over the edge. Taking supplements does that occasionally. I cry as I swallow them, thinking of how you always cared enough for me to make sure I was getting the right nutrients. Other times, taking the supplements brings me comfort for the very same reason.

I still can't eat the meals we ate together, so mostly I'm snacking. Just what I need, right? I usually have a salad though, so that's good. I have a craving for your chili, but I'll probably never eat it again. It won't taste the same—I never could make it the way you did—and it would make me too sad.

It's been nice visiting with you here—I wish it were for real and not just in memory. I think often of how brave you were. I need to be brave, too. I thought I'd just need courage to get through the final stages of your illness and the first months of grieving, but now I know I'm going to need courage to live the rest of my life without you.

I love you, Jeff. I hope you're well. Adios, compadre.

Day 165, **Dear Jeff,**

People keep telling me that you're in a better place, but that I have to get on with my life because life is a gift. Huh? If you're in a better place, why aren't I there? If life is a gift, why was it taken from you?

I still can't figure out the point of it all. Is there anything universally important? Love, perhaps, but not everyone loves or is loved. Creativity? But not everyone is creative. Truth? But what is truth? If nothing is universally important, does anything matter? You're probably tired of this constant questioning, but your death has posed such a conundrum for me that I'm totally lost. I need to find the bedrock of life, a foundation on which to rebuild my life.

I had no idea I had all these tears in me. The drops are huge, like a badly dripping faucet. I am still stunned by the depth and breadth of my grief. I grieve for the good times and the bad. I grieve for what I got from our relationship and what I didn't. I grieve for me, what I've lost, and what I'll never have. I grieve for you and all you lost, all you never had, all you never will have. I grieve for that young man, that radiant man I met so many years ago because I know the end of his story. And I grieve for the man whose life was cut short.

It can't be normal, this protracted grief, but people in the grief business keep assuring me I'm doing well.

I hope you're doing well, too. I love you. I always will.

Day 176, Blog Post, **Is Twenty-Five Weeks a Long Time or a Little Time?**

Is twenty-five weeks a long time or a little time? I haven't a clue. All I know is that twenty-five weeks ago my life mate—my soul mate—died of inoperable kidney cancer, and I am still learning to deal with his absence. Sometimes it seems as if he's been gone forever, and other times it feels as if he just left, as if I should be able to reach out, hold him in my arms, and keep him safe. Strange, that—I couldn't stop his dying when he was living it. I certainly can't stop it now that he is gone.

When I was a child, twenty-five weeks seemed a lifetime, especially if I was counting down to Christmas or summer vacation. When the weight of age began settling on my shoulders, twenty-five weeks went by in a flash. Or at least they used to. Now weeks stop and go, dam and flow, and I no longer have a concept of time, perhaps because the passing weeks are not relative to anything but his death and my loss.

Even the future seems long and short by turns. I think of growing old by myself, of learning to live with the limitations aging will bring, and ultimately of dying alone, and the coming years seem long. Yet those same years will still be full of life, maybe even happiness, which will make them feel short.

I do know that twenty-five weeks is a long time when it comes to feeling lost, alone, and confused by this major change—both his and mine. (I am very confused by his death. I worry about him still, feel sad for what he is missing, glad he is beyond pain.) At the same time, twenty-five weeks is way too short to even begin to process all that this experience means and will mean.

So, is twenty-five weeks a long time or a little time? I haven't a clue.

Day 185, Blog Post, I am a Six-Month Grief Survivor

Six months ago my life mate—my soul mate—died of kidney cancer, and my life changed forever. I survived the first excruciating weeks, and now I am learning to live with his absence and finding ways of going on by myself, but it's lonely. So few people know how to act around the bereft, and they end up offering us maxims that bring no comfort because the adages are simply not true.

People tell us that time heals. Time does *not* heal. We heal. Grief helps us heal. Time does nothing. Time doesn't even pass—we pass through time like persons passing through an endless desert.

People tell us that we'll get over our loss, but when you have suffered a soul-quaking loss, you never totally get over it. Nor do you want to. Getting over it seems like a betrayal, a negation of the life you shared. The best you can do is eventually accept the person's absence as a part of your life.

People tell us to get on with life. They don't understand that this *is* our life. Grief is how we get on with it.

Grief is not the problem. The problem is that our loved one died. Grief is the way we deal with that loss, the way we process it, the way we heal the wound of amputation. By experiencing the pain, by allowing ourselves to feel the loss, we honor our loved one and our relationship, and gradually we move through the pain to . . . to what? I'm not sure what lies on the other side of grief. I've passed the worst of the pain but not yet arrived at a new way of living.

During these past six months, I've been inundated with information about how to deal with grief. I purposely refrained from reading the material, which is strange for me—I've always been one who researches everything—but I didn't want to know the accepted way to grieve. I wanted to experience my own grief without the current fad getting in the way. It used to be that grief was a regimented experience—one wore black and mourned for a year. More recently, the "stages of grief" became the accepted way of grieving, though now there are various new ways of thinking about grief. The truth is, grief is personal, and except for the extremes of not allowing oneself to feel anything and trying to find ways of dying so you can join your loved one, however you grieve, that is the right way to grieve.

Grief makes even friends and family uncomfortable, so eventually the bereft learn to hide what they feel. They stop talking about their loved one, but they never forget.

I will never forget.

He will always live in my memory.

Seventh Month

Day 197, **Dear Jeff,**

It's been a while since I've written, but I've been thinking about you. Are you glad you're dead? You said you were ready to die, to be done with your suffering, yet at the very end you seemed reluctant to go.

I didn't want to throw you away. Despite all the problems with your restlessness and the disorientation from the drugs, I wasn't ready for you to leave me. I still am not. Nor do I want to go back to where we were that last year, waiting for you to die. We were both so miserable, but honestly, this is even worse. I can live without you. The problem is, I don't want to, and I don't see why I have to.

I want to come home. Please, can I come home? I have a good place to stay, but without you, I feel homeless. Sometimes I watch movies from your collection and imagine you're watching with me, but that makes me cry because I know you're not here. Your ashes are, but you're not.

I broke a cup today, one more thing gone out of the life we shared. Our stuff is going to break, wear out, get used up. I'll replace some of it, add new things, write new books, and it will dilute what we shared. Is there going to be anything left of "us"? I feel uncomfortable in this new skin, this new life, as if it's not mine. As if I'm wearing clothes too big and too small all at the same time.

There's so much I hate about your being gone—hate it for me and hate it for you. It might be easier if I knew you were glad to be dead, but so far you've been mum about your situation. Just one more thing to hate—the silence of the grave. (Well, the silence of the funerary urn.)

Adios, compadre. If you get a chance, let me know you're okay.

Day 200, Blog Post, **Is Hate a Stage of Grief?**

Is hate a stage of grief? If not, it should be. I don't see

how one can avoid it.

I've proved, to myself at least, that I can live without my life mate. It's been twenty-eight weeks since he died, and in that time I've managed to get rid of his clothes and his car, clean out the accumulation of decades, move 1000 miles from our home, walk at least that many miles, eat, drink a lot of water, sleep (after a fashion), make new friends (mostly people who have also lost their mates, which gives us an instant bond of understanding). I smile now, and laugh. I can even look forward to the immediate future: I've planned an excursion (going to an art museum to see Mesoamerican antiquities, including an Olmec head) and I'm thinking about doing NaNoWriMo (National Novel Writing Month), something I said I would never do, but I need to kick start my writing after all the kicks life has given me lately. The point is, despite my grief, despite the oceans of tears I've shed and continue to shed, I have done these things. I can live without him. But I hate that I have to.

I'm coming to an acceptance of his death, though I'm not sure I understand it. (Don't much understand life, either, but that's a topic for another day.) I know I will never see him again in this life, and I hate it. I hate that I will never go back home to him. I hate that I will never talk to him again. I hate that I will never see his slow sweet smile again.

I hate that he will never watch another movie. I hate that he will never plant another tree and watch it grow. I hate that he will never have another cat. I hate that he will never read another book. I hate that he will never listen to his music tapes again. I hate that he will never start another business. I hate that he will never play another game of baseball or smell another flower or swim in another lake. I hate that so many of his dreams are going unfulfilled.

Most of all, I hate that he is dead.

I am thankful that I had him in my life for as long as I did, but I hate that his years were cut short. I know I should be glad that he isn't suffering any more, and I am. But I hate that he had to suffer in the first place.

This stage will pass as have all the other stages of grief

I've lived through. I might even find happiness again, but he will still be gone. And I hate that.

Day 202, **Dear Jeff,**

For the first time since you died, I almost forgot to advance your permanent calendar. I'm surprised I've remembered to do it all these months. I thought it would be a remembrance, but I don't need anything to remind me of you—everything I see, say, do reminds me of you.

I've decided the only way to fill the hole you left in my life, to make sense of your absence, is to fill it with activities I would not have done if you were alive. There are not enough events in the whole world to fill the void, but I need to try, otherwise I'll never manage to get through the next decades. I hope I don't become one of those people who hold on to their pain because it's all they have to make them feel alive, but it is all I have to connect to you. Well, I have memories and some of your things, but that's not enough.

Would your death be easier to accept if you'd been happy? Is your unhappiness a reason for me to accept your death? What makes this so confusing is that your long dying, the accumulating weakness and pain made you unhappy, so how can I use that as a rationale for being okay with your dying?

I'm like a child, wanting to scream, "It's unfair!" And it is, but that doesn't change the fact that you're dead.

Did I hold your hand when you died? I think I just stood there as you took your last breath, but I don't remember. I don't remember much of the last couple of years. It's like I was in suspended animation, just waiting for you to die. What a terrible thing to say, but it was a terrible time to have lived through. But you didn't live through it, did you? Well, you did live it, you just didn't survive it.

I wonder if subconsciously I knew all this pain was waiting for me, and that's why I closed myself off from the reality of your dying. I don't like this, Jeff. I don't like it at all.

Day 204, **Grief Journal**

I struggle to see the truth of life and death. Supposedly, you can have a relationship with someone after they are dead, but it's all in the mind, in memory. What's the difference between that and fantasy? And how much of life is lived in the mind? All of it? All except the present? But even the present is lived in the mind since the mind (or rather the brain) takes the waves of nothingness and transforms them into somethingness. So what is reality? The intersection of all minds?

If life really is so immense and wonderful, how come we couldn't come up with anything better than the silliness of everyday life—houses, cars, television, *things.*

I don't pretend to understand, though I do try. Foolishly, perhaps. Is the human mind, with its finiteness, capable of understanding the truth? Now that Jeff is beyond his mind, beyond the limits of his physical brain, does he understand? Does he know? Does he still exist on some level?

I try to comprehend all he went through, and my heart aches for him. I have many regrets on his behalf, but I doubt he has them, especially if he is oblivious. (In oblivion?) I can see now I have to let those regrets go—they are not part of my present, though in a way he is. He is in my memory, in my cells' memory, my soul's memory. And isn't his pain a part of him? Do I diminish his life by moving beyond his pain?

I never knew grief could be so difficult, but it wouldn't be hard if he were here to share it with me as he shared so much else. I still cry for him. I miss what we had, what we never had, what we never will have.

Day 206, Blog Post, **Many Shades of Grief**

When you lose someone significant in your life, someone whose very being has helped define you in some way, grief can be overwhelming. So many stages and shades of grief bombard you that at times you think you are going crazy—but except for the very extremes of grief—mummifying yourself so you don't feel anything for years on end or

93

saving pills so you can end your life—chances are what you are feeling is normal.

Many people who try to deal with the loss completely on their own have no idea if what they are feeling is normal. When you lose your husband, your daughter also loses her father, your sister-in-law loses her brother, your neighbor loses his friend. At first, you grieve together, but one by one everyone else puts aside their grief until you are the only one left crying. And they begin to hint that you need therapy. They got over their pain, why can't you? After all, you all lost the same man. But you didn't have the same relationship, so you won't experience the same shades of grief.

I was in such pain after losing my life mate that I decided to go to a grief support group, hoping they could tell me how to survive the agony. I was afraid, at first, that I would be overwhelmed by everyone else's pain; instead, I found a group of people who knew what I was going through, who listened to my sad story and who, because of their own survival, let me know that I would survive. And that was comforting. I also learned that the only way to survive the pain is to go through the process of grieving.

It's the hardest thing I have ever done, embracing grief.

Grief takes you to the ends of your limits. It makes you question everything you thought you knew about life, about yourself, about death. It can make you scream at the heavens, make you cry until you think you're drowning in your own tears, make you want not to live. All this is accompanied by a host of physical symptoms, such as dizziness, tightness in the chest, restlessness, irritability, inability to focus or organize, inability to eat or sleep (or to eat and sleep too much). And when you think you've cried all your tears, finished with your panic attacks, come to accept that he isn't coming back, grief returns, but this time it comes in a different shade, perhaps not so black as in the beginning, but still dark.

Right now I'm going through a time of pearl gray days scattered with storm-cloud gray moments. Though I've done the work of grief in my own way, I have had one great benefit that many people don't have—that grief support group. Because of their support, because I know someone is paying attention, I have felt free to embrace my grief fully without worrying that I'm crazy or that I need therapy. Because of them, I know I am coping well, I know my grief is normal, I know I am completely sane. I just haven't finished with my grieving yet, and it's possible that I may never be completely finished. And that too is normal.

Day 211, Blog Post, **Grief: Cleaning Up the Past**
Thirty weeks and still counting. I've already stopped counting the days since my life mate—my soul mate—died, soon I'll stop counting the weeks, and eventually I'll stop counting the months. Perhaps there will even come a time when the anniversary of his death goes unnoticed. But in the end, it doesn't matter. Whatever happens in my life, he will always be a part of it—almost everything I do, feel, say relates to him in some way. He was instrumental in making me who I am, and his death is the catalyst to make me who I will become, though I still don't feel different from who I was before he died. So much of the change in me came before his death, during the long years of his dying.

During the last year of his life, as the cancer spread from his kidney up to his brain, he spent more and more time alone. I thought I coped well with the situation, continuing with my life, taking his dying for granted. I thought I'd moved on. In fact, I told him I'd be okay after he was gone, that I'd finished with my grieving. And I believed it.

After he died, the depth of my grief stunned me. His death shattered my state of suspended animation, and I was appalled by the way I'd behaved that last year. How could I possibly have taken his dying for granted? How could I have refused to see what he was feeling? How could I have become impatient with his growing weakness, his reclusiveness, his inability to carry on the long ping-ponging conversations that had characterized our relationship? How could I not have treasured his every word? Even after his diagnosis, even after we'd apologized for any wrongs, even after we become as close as we had been at the beginning, I continued to think I wouldn't grieve. How could I have not known how much I still loved him?

I'd been living that last year over and over again in memory, trying to make it come out right, but no matter what I did, I could not change the past. It haunted me, that year. I could feel everything I refused to feel back then, and it about crushed me. A few days ago, while I was crying uncontrollably, I remembered hearing something during my grief support group session that struck a bell, so I checked back over the paper the counselor had read to us. "Self protection—denying the meaning of the loss." Aha!

I had never denied his dying, just the immediacy of it. (Which is not surprising. He had the strongest determination of anyone I'd ever met, and he kept rallying until he couldn't rally anymore.) But unconsciously (or subconsciously), I had denied what his death would mean to me. Denied what he meant to me.

After my aha moment, I started wondering what would have happened if I hadn't gone into suspended animation, and I realized if, during that last year, I had let myself see what he was feeling, let myself feel what his dying and his death would mean to me, I would have been in such agony I would have cried all the time. He would have hated that he was causing me so much pain, which would have made me feel even worse. I still couldn't have done anything for him, so eventually I would have blocked out all that was happening. I would have gone on with my own life and left his dying to him. I would have become impatient with the restrictions of our life, with his weakness, with his retreat into himself. In other words, even if I could have gone back and relived that year knowing the truth of it, my behavior would have been the same. And he would still have died.

With that realization, my tears stopped. I continue to have teary moments, but I am at peace with the way I acted that last year of his life. I still wish I could have done something to make that last year easier for him, of course, but perhaps I did—with all his troubles, at least he didn't have to deal with my grief.

Day 212, **Dear Jeff,**

It's sort of pathetic to keep writing to you. I'm not sure who I'm writing to—to me, to my memory of you, to that spark of energy that was you and is now absorbed into the whole? I suppose it would be even more pathetic if you were hanging around waiting to hear from me. Even if there is some sort of life after death, I don't imagine we will ever be together again. Forever is a long, long time and the universe is vast. Would we even recognize each other? Could be. Somehow I recognized you when we met, though I don't know what I recognized—the eternal you or a person who matched a template in my mind? (I was going to say "in my heart," but you and I know a heart doesn't feel. It's merely a pump.)

Now that the worst of my grief has passed, I feel empty. So much of what I've been feeling lately was not grief at your death, but grief at your dying. I feel bad that we didn't spend a lot of time together that year, but it might have been a good thing. What was there to share except our pain?

I'll probably spend the rest of my life puzzling out the meaning of us—our connection, your influence on my life, our current situation (you dead, me alive).

I wish we could meet somewhere, maybe at Hardee's in Love's Park, or the lake in Minoqua, or the mountains by Bear Creek, and talk about all that has happened. You could tell me about your last year, about dying, about being dead. I could tell you about grieving. We could cry together, hug each other, be together without pretense or denial.

I worry that I'll forget you—I haven't a good memory for faces, and specific moments get lost in the jumble of years, but maybe when I'm old we'll be reunited in memory. For the aged, the past is often more real than the present. I hope the past I remember is our past, not my earlier years. I'd love to relive those years at your store, to meet you once again when you were young and strong and healthy and radiant.

The end was so miserable, I forget what joy you brought to my life. Even if I start to forget you, I will always miss you. Is that a good thing? I don't know. It is what is. Adios, compadre. I love you.

Day 213, **Dear Jeff,**
It's early, a little after 6:00am, but I just dreamed about you and wanted to get it written down so I'd remember. In the dream, I was walking down a city street and caught a flash of your car as it passed an intersection a block away. Since I knew you'd eventually have to turn onto the street where I was, I kept turning around to look for you, and I saw you—you were driving away from me. I waved at you, but you were staring straight ahead and I didn't think you saw me. Then, as I rounded the block, you pulled up to the curb a few feet from the corner, and waited for me. You smiled at me. I hurried to the car, but woke before I got in.

I smiled when I woke, thinking of you, and I'm smiling still. It was wonderful seeing you, Jeff, if only in my dreams.

Day 214, **Grief Journal**
Life/death has me very confused. I still don't see that a person lives after they are dead. What survives, if anything? The part of us we never knew—the un-sub-conscious? If so, how would we know who we were after we were dead? Is it just the energy in our bodies that is released? If so, for sure we would not know who we were.

On the other hand, without some sort of afterlife, life simply does not make sense. What's the point of it all? To survive? For what—more survival until there is no more survival? To help others? Why? So they can survive? For what?

If there is life after death, what do you do with eternity? You have no ears to hear music, no eyes to read or watch a movie, no legs to walk, no hands to caress another, no mouth to talk, no brain to think. Sounds like a horror movie to me. And what will we do if Jeff and I meet again? Bask in each other's light? That would get boring after a minute or two.

I guess it doesn't really matter. Whether life ends or continues after death, this is where I am now. So what do I want from the rest of my life? I don't know. I've never really wanted much. I never even wanted happiness—I thought other things were more important, such as truth. But now? I truly do not know what I want, except that which I cannot have. I yearn desperately to talk to Jeff—not about anything in particular, just to talk. It's like a voice hunger, or a word hunger. A dozen times a day I think of something I want to say to him, to ask him, to marvel at. Sometimes I just want the feeling of connection. I still yearn to put my arms around him and protect him from what will happen, but it's already happened, and anyway, my touch never had the power to heal.

I know I'm strong enough to handle this—after all, I am handling it—but I DON'T WANT TO!!

Day 215, Blog Post, **I Am a Seven-Month Grief Survivor**

Grief is so encompassing that for months my thoughts focused entirely on my dead mate—my soul mate—reinforcing my idea that falling in love and experiencing grief are the bookends of a shared life. When we were together, he was so often by my side as we ran errands, fixed meals, watched movies, talked for hours on end, that I didn't need to focus on him—he was there. And then he wasn't.

In the movie *The Butcher's Wife,* Demi Moore talks about searching for her split apart. Very romantic this idea of finding your split apart, but what happens when your split apart is split apart from you once more? I can tell you—it releases such a storm of emotion that you feel as if you will never find yourself again, that you will be forever swept away in the tsunami/hurricane/soulquake that is new grief.

I've weathered seven months of grief, from the first global storm to the more isolated mists that beset me now. I'm settling back into myself, letting go of the incredible tension that grief brings. We bereft are so focused on our lost one, so tensed against hurtful memories and mementoes, that it can bring on a host of physical problems, including Post

Traumatic Stress Syndrome.

I am lucky. I've been able to release this tension through walks, through tears, and—at the beginning—through screaming. I have not passed all the landmarks of grief—some people experience their worst pain at eight months, others need two years just to regain their equilibrium, and of course, there are all those firsts that are yet to come: the first Thanksgiving, first Christmas, first anniversary of his death—but perhaps the worst of the storms have passed. Or I could be fooling myself. This sad but not terribly painful stage I am going through could be just a hiatus, the eye of a storm, and the forces of grief are gathering themselves for a new onslaught. These months of grief survival, however, have taught me that I will be able to endure whatever comes.

I thought I'd be different after going through such storms of grief, (shouldn't I be?) but I feel as if I am still myself, or rather, I feel as if I am myself again. I am sadder, of course, and that sadness will probably always shadow any future happiness, which is as it should be. One can never unknow such trauma. It will always be part of me.

He will always be part of me.

In many ways, he gave me life. He made me feel that life was worth living because he was in it. I have to learn to feel that life is worth living because *I* am in it, and that will be a long time coming. I am still at the stage where I don't care if I live. NO, I am *not* suicidal. I am not stockpiling pills or thinking suicidal thoughts. This not caring is perhaps one of the longest-lived stages of grief, one that we bereft only talk about to each other—or our counselors—because it is so often misunderstood by those who have not been in a similar situation. One thing that keeps me going is curiosity about where life will take me now that he is not here for me to love.

Where does that love go when it is no longer needed? I don't know. I do know that when you love someone, their well-being is as important to you as your own, and then suddenly that someone is gone, leaving behind those unfulfilled feelings of wanting to help. Of caring. Of empathy. I still think of him almost all the time, still wish I could put my arms around him and make him well. When I hear a noise, sometimes I think it is he, and my first inclination is to go to him. When I hear or see something that would amuse or outrage him, sometimes I get up to go tell him. But these thoughts and actions are not as painful as they once were.

I have survived seven months of grief. I will continue to survive.

Eighth Month

Day 221, Blog Post, **The Simple Truth**

I'm beginning to understand the truth of grief—you never truly get over it. Whenever I think I've reached a stage of acceptance and peace, grief has a way of swinging around and coming at me from a different direction, and it always takes me by surprise.

Yesterday was a good day. I started in on my novel for NaNoWriMo and managed to write the allotted number of words in just a few hours, which pleased me. I'm such a slow writer, I thought it would take me all day to do it, especially since I piddled around for a while, trying to decide which kind of paper to use, which pencil, which clipboard. (Yeah, I admit it—I still write by hand, mainly because it's easier on my eyes.)

I also posted a blog for the first day of NaBloPoMo (National Blog Posting Month).

My self-imposed commitments finished for the day, I went walking in the desert. It was perfect weather—blue skies and warm, still air.

Then bam! Out of nowhere, grief socked me in the gut. I wanted so much to see my mate, to talk to him, that I would barely breathe. The pain lasted for hours. And tears? Too many to count.

The novel I started writing for NaNo was about a grieving woman, so perhaps that had something to do with my upsurge in grief. I've been worried that immersing myself in the story of a woman who lost her husband might be a bit much for me at this stage, but I also know that I won't want to revisit grief once I'm done with it. (Yes, I know—one is never done with grief, but the pain does lessen and the bouts of tears come further apart.)

It's possible any writing would have brought on this re-grief—he was my sounding board (literally a sounding board—I always read to him what I wrote). And it's possible it was just time. Lately I've been distracting myself when the pain crept in, so it could have been building up.

The whys of this spate of grief, however, are not important. It still comes down to the simple truth: He is dead and there's not a damn thing I can do about it except learn to live with it.

Day 222, Blog Post, **How to Respond to "How Are You?"**

A month or so ago, a Facebook friend, another woman who lost her mate, suggested I write a blog on what to say when people ask a griever, "How are you?" When I first realized that people were losing interest in my sad tale and didn't really want a truthful answer, I asked a bereavement counselor that very question. She said a good response is, "I'm coping," which is the response I used for a few months. Now I just say, "I'm okay." Even if I'm not okay, I tell people I'm okay. Or if I'm being polite, I say, "I'm fine, how are you?" There is nothing wrong with that—it's a rote response to a rote question. Most people who ask how you are do not especially want to know. It's an accepted conversation starter, a way for people to show token interest so they can move on to more exciting topics—themselves, for example.

Someone who comes back at you with, "No, really, how are you?" is someone who deserves no response at all, especially if they add, "this is me, remember?" If they need to remind you who they are, you don't know them well enough to tell the truth. Besides, if you wanted to tell the person how you really were, you would have already done so.

People who truly care will ask a more specific question: "Did you sleep well," for example, or . . . I don't know. Any question that shows genuine interest will suffice, and those you can respond to honestly if you wish. Or not. In the end, your grief is your business. People do not need to know you are still crying yourself to sleep every night, or that you miss him so much you can feel it like an ache in your bones, or that the world feels as if it's aslant now that he is gone.

Unless you want them to know, that is.

Even at the best of times, "How are you?" is a question without any response except "I'm fine," or "I'm okay." It always makes me wonder, "How am I in relation to what?" Are they asking about my health, my state of mind, my finances? With grief added into the equation, I wonder if they are asking how I am in relation to the way I was before he died, in relation to the way I felt immediately after his death, or in relation to nothing at all.

I have to admit, like everyone else, I usually ask the question, but as a part of the greeting, "Hi! How are you?" I don't mind if someone comes back at me with, "I'm fine, how are you?" because that is the ritual. Once that is out of the way, we can settle down to a serious discussion. If the person is another griever, I don't expect an in-depth response, I *know* how they are doing.

So, to recap a rather wordy and convoluted post, if someone asks how you are, "fine" is fine.

Day 226, Blog Post, **Desert Revelation**

While walking in the desert this morning, I had a vision. Well, not a vision so much as a revelation.

I'd been thinking about my grieving woman novel, my work-in-progress, which is shaping up to be the story of a woman in search of herself. She is directionless after her loss, has a lot of unfinished business to take care of, and is trying to figure out who she is now that she is no longer a wife. I wondered if people would accept that this woman is finding out all sorts of things about herself that she didn't know—after all, a person in her early fifties should have some idea of who she is.

Then I realized that even if we have a strong identity and know almost everything there is to know about ourselves, it's still possible and perhaps necessary to revise our self-concept, especially after going through a trauma such as a major loss.

I saw that our psyches are like nesting dolls or boxes within boxes or doors within doors (choose your cliché).

You never see the doors, so you think you know who you are, but a great emotional upheaval can cause a door to open, letting you see more of yourself and what you are capable of, revealing a part of your identity that might have been hidden from you until that moment.

You get to know who you now are, adding to or changing your idea of yourself, rethinking the past in light of this new awareness. You get comfortable with this revised self-concept and then BAM! More trauma, and another door. You never have to go through the door, of course, but if you do, you might find riches of which you were unaware.

What can I say? It was the desert. Wandering in the desert is traditionally a place for both sun-induced absurdities and great insights.

Day 228, Blog Post, *Healing the Split in Ourselves*

I've spent many hours walking in the desert during the past few months, which has given me plenty of time to contemplate grief, life, death and anything else that comes to mind. One thought that filtered through my mind was the idea that when my mate died, I split in two. The me that shared a life with him is grieving still, while the other me, the one who was born with his death, continues to live and grow. As long as I am in the person of this second me, I do fine—I'm strong, in control of my emotions, looking forward to what comes to me in life. The problem is that I keep slipping over to the other me, the grieving me, and when I do, the grief is as new as it was when it first hit me. The task is to reconnect the two parts—both the grieving me and the new me.

This might seem like dissociative personality disorder, though it's not really a disorder. It's how we all deal with life. I don't remember the name of the person, but a psychologist once hypothesized that there are no true moods. What we think of as moods are different personalities. This natural order becomes a disorder when you lose track of yourself during mood swings or when they cease to be a way of dealing with life and become a way of hiding from life. I don't know the truth of this, nor do I know the truth of my idea of splitting apart, but my idea feels true. I can almost feel the clunk of the gears as I switch from one mode to the other. I don't switch as often now, which makes me think I'll eventually be whole again.

Today, at my grief group meeting, I had a graphic example of how I am moving beyond my grief (at least for the moment. It does swing back and slam me in the gut from time to time).

During these meetings, there is a lesson—a topic—that we discuss before going on to personal updates. One of today's lessons started out: *Grief brings with it a terrible and lonely loss.* Instead of acknowledging the sentiment, and contemplating my terrible and lonely loss as I was supposed to, I looked at the words, and said, "No, it doesn't."

This brought the meeting to a standstill while everyone stared at me.

"Grief doesn't bring the loss. Loss brings the grief," I said.

More silence. Eventually, they agreed with me, probably to shut me up and get the discussion going again.

The point is, I focused on the words, not on the emotion. Of course, this could be more that I'm in writing mode than that I'm moving on with my life, but I took it as a good sign. Because this is the truth: death brings a terrible and lonely loss. Grief is our reaction to the loss, and ultimately it's how we learn to heal the rift in ourselves brought about by that loss.

Day 233, Blog Post, **Grief: All Things Considered . . .**
Another Saturday gone, thirty-three of them since my life mate died. Saturday—his death day—always makes me sad. Even if I'm not consciously aware of the day, my body still reacts, as if it's been marking the passing weeks. For some reason grief hit me hard this past Saturday. Perhaps it was the lovely weather we've been having, weather he will never enjoy. Perhaps it was the homesickness for him that has been growing in me again. Perhaps it was just time for another

bout of tears to relieve the growing tension of dealing with his absence. Grief doesn't need a reason, though. Grief has an agenda of its own and comes when it wishes.

I've been mostly doing okay, moving on with my life—walking in the desert, writing, blogging and doing various internet activities, making friends both online and offline—but nothing, not even my hard-won acceptance changes the fact that he is dead. At times I still have trouble understanding his sheer goneness. My mind doesn't seem to be able to make that leap, though I am getting used to his not being around. I don't like it, but I am getting used to it. Maybe that's the best I will ever be able to do.

Someone asked me the other day how I was doing. "I'm doing okay all things considered," I responded. His witty and wise response: "Then don't consider all things."

I've been taking his advice, and trying not to consider all things—trying to consider just enough to get through the day, especially on Saturday.

I don't expect much of myself on Saturdays. Often, I spend the afternoon and evening watching movies my life mate taped for us. It makes me feel as if we are together, if only for a few brief delusional minutes. I try not to consider that he'll never watch his tapes again. I try not to consider the long lonely years stretching before me. I try not to consider that I'll never see his smile again, or hear his laugh. I concentrate on the movies, and so Saturday passes.

By Sunday, I usually regain a modicum of equanimity, but Saturday always comes around again.

Day 234, **Dear Jeff,**

I'm not doing well at all. Haven't been able to stop crying for the past three days. How am I supposed to deal with your being gone? I've been crying in the desert again, calling out for you, talking to you. I thought I'd gotten past that—had a week or two of peace, and then my anguish started up again. I don't want to get to where I'm okay with your being dead, but I don't want to be crying all the time, either.

Every once in a while I feel as if we're still together, just in different rooms, but I'm deluding myself. Not that such a delusion is wrong, but when the truth hits me again, it's like new.

What a stupid thing this is—life and death. People who say all things are possible are idiots. If all things were possible, we'd be together. We belong together. Now I belong only to me. And it's not enough. I know I sound whiney and self-pitying, and there's a good reason for that. I *am* whiney and self-pitying.

I'm tired of tears, of pain, of missing you. The only way to stop all that is to be with you. But you're dead. What a ridiculous situation.

Adios, compadre. Take care of yourself.

Day 235, Blog Post, **Grief: Denying Denial**
I never really had a choice about feeling my grief. It wasn't so much that I embraced it, but that it embraced me. It took hold of my life and didn't let go, though it is easing enough so that I am able to see the process for what it is.

People talk about denial as if it's a bad thing. If I'd been able to deny grief and just go on living as if my mate of thirty-four years hadn't died, I'd probably have done so. Grief is debilitating, disorienting, causes innumerable physical and emotional reactions, makes one susceptible to cancer, accidents, and other close-to-death encounters and on top of that, it's just downright painful.

So why deny denial? Because in the end, it's better to embrace grief, to learn to live with the pain (which does diminish, though according to comments left on my blog from others who have also lost their mates, it never goes away completely. It can resurface even years later). By embracing grief, by learning how to cope with it, you can learn how to feel deeply again, look forward to the future, and embrace life. This in no way negates your loss, but allows you to honor his death with your life.

Another reason to deny denial is that grief will affect you whether you embrace it or not, but the effects of denied grief are not overt ones such as crying, eating too much or too little, sleeping too much or too little, feeling as if you've been kicked in the gut, feeling as if half your heart is missing. Instead, grief that goes underground can create in you long-term problems, including the symptoms of post-traumatic-stress disorder. Two friends—both of whom lost their husbands a few month ago, both of whom are deluged with family and family obligations that give them no time to grieve—were diagnosed with PTSD after days of internal quivering that only responded to drugs. They do not have time to spare for grief, but grief is not sparing them.

Grief is stressful, which is why crying, screaming, beating up on defenseless sofas are necessary—they help relieve that pent-up stress. You can go into denial and hold grief in, but it's like holding in your stomach for years on end—you can never think of anything else but your stomach. If you hold yourself tightly against memories, dreams, unexpected encounters with photos, you have no time for living. Perhaps you don't see a purpose for living now, but if you do your grief work (and grief is work, there's no doubt about that) chances are you will regain your desire to live. You might even be able to love fully again, and that means risking more pain, but after dealing with your grief, you will be strong enough to accept the risk.

At least, that's the way I've interpreted the grief process. You might see different reasons for either denying grief or denying denial.

Day 240, **Dear Jeff,**

I wish I could talk to you, hug you, take away your pain. I know your pain is gone now, but if, as people tell me, you still live in my memory, then you are still in pain because I remember it. I feel as if I failed you.

Odd that the bereft often get angry at the dead for dying. I'm not angry at you, though occasionally I get angry at the situation. I miss you more than I ever thought possible. The world does not feel the same without you. I'm starting to let go of the tension of my grief and the emotions of the last year, and am relaxing into myself more, which is why I'm still feeling our separation—I feel the subtleties. I love you, Jeff. Take care of yourself.

Day 244, Blog Post, **Grateful Even in Grief (Thanksgiving Day)**

I thought I had nothing for which to be grateful this Thanksgiving, then it struck me how wrong I was. I have a lot to be grateful for despite my continued (though much gentler) grief.

I am thankful I have a place to sleep, food to eat, desert trails to walk, books to read, words to write.

I am thankful for the people who have entered my life to give me support during this bleak time.

I am thankful I had my life mate to love and care for.

I am thankful my life mate loved and cared for me.

I am thankful for the emotional security offered by our relationship, which gave me the freedom to try new things.

I am thankful he shared his life—and his death—with me.

I am thankful for our added closeness at the end.

I am thankful he is no longer suffering.

I am thankful he didn't linger as a helpless invalid. He dreaded that.

I am thankful for his legacy. He faced his death with such courage that he gave me the courage to face my life.

I am even thankful for my grief. It reminds me that he shared part of this journey called life with me, and it is helping me become the person I need to be to continue my journey alone.

So, this Thanksgiving, I am grateful even in grief.

Day 245, **Dear Jeff,**

Last night I watched *The Last Dance*, the Eric Stoltz and Maureen O'Hara movie you edited to get rid of the flash-backs. I cried all the way through. When I'm old, will I still be missing you? I don't want to do this, Jeff. I don't want to be this broken person. And I do feel broken, as if parts of me are missing.

I didn't expect to still be crying for you after eight

months, but sometimes your death is so fresh in my mind I feel as if I just lost you. It's starting to sink in that my sorrow doesn't affect you. You don't need it. It's almost impossible for me to comprehend that I'll never see you again. It's almost impossible to comprehend the sheer loneliness of my life and the aloneness that's in store for me.

I want to come home, Jeff. I want to talk to you once more. How can I be this person—this heartbroken, soul-broken person? I thought I was stronger than this. I thought we'd always be together. I miss you. Take care of yourself.

Day 245, **Dear Jeff,**

Same day, a few minutes later. I don't want to get up and start my day. I want to continue this connection with you, as one-sided as it might be.

One thing Maureen O'Hara said in *The Last Dance* was that she loved Charlie because he always listened. It's what I loved about you, too, and why I felt we'd grown apart that last year—you couldn't listen any more. You could barely hear, barely stand, barely get through the days. I'd already lost you by then—not to death, but to your dying. It was something we couldn't share, just as my grief is something we can't share.

I better get up, go for a walk. Just one more thing we can no longer share. Adios, compadre.

Day 246, Blog Post, **I Am an Eight-Month Grief Survivor**

When you love someone deeply, their well-being is as important to you as your own, but what do you do with that feeling when your someone is gone? Eight months ago, my life mate died, and now he has no need for stories to amuse or outrage him, no need for tasty meals to tempt his appetite, no need for comfort or caring or kindness, and yet my habit of thinking of him remains. Eventually, I imagine, the habit will wear itself out, but for now I still find myself thinking of ways to make his life a bit easier or a bit more enjoyable.

After eight months, I am still in . . . not shock, exactly, but a state of non-comprehension. I can't comprehend his death, his sheer goneness. I can't comprehend his life, though perhaps that is not for me to bother about. Most of all, I can't comprehend my sorrow. I never saw much reason for grief. Someone died, you moved on. Period. I thought I was too stoic, too practical to mourn, and yet, here I am, still grieving for someone who has no need for my sorrow.

Despite my continued grief, I am moving on. My sporadic tears do not stop me from accomplishing the goals I set myself, such as NaNoWriMo and daily walks. My sorrow doesn't keep me from taking care of myself—or mostly taking care of myself. (I don't always eat right, and I don't always sleep well.) Moving on, as I have learned, is not about abandoning one's grief, but moving on despite the grief.

Grief is much gentler on me now, and I can sidestep it by turning my mind to other things, but I don't always want to. I have not yet reached the point where thoughts of him bring me only happiness, and I need to remember him. If tears and pain are still part of that remembrance, so be it.

We shared our lives, our thoughts, our words—we talked about everything, often from morning to night—yet even before he died, we started going separate ways, he toward his death, me toward continued life. I often wonder what he would think of my grief, but just as his life is not for me to try to comprehend, my grief does not belong to him. It is mine alone.

And so the months pass, eight now. Soon it will be a year. Sometimes it feels as if he died only days ago, and I expect him to call and tell me I can come home—I've proven that I can live without him, so I don't have to continue to do so. Sometimes it feels as if he's been gone forever, that our life together wasn't real, perhaps something I conjured up out of the depths of my loneliness. Sometimes my grief doesn't even feel real, and I worry that I've created it out of a misguided need for self-importance. Such are the ways of grief, this strange and magical thinking. This could be magical thinking, too, but it seems to me that having survived eight months of grief, I can survive anything.

Ninth Month

Day 249, Blog Post, **Owing His Memory?**

In a novel I just finished reading, I found a graphic example of why I write about grieving—so few understand the nature of grief. In the book, the author talked about a character who had been running drugs, and because of it, his girlfriend owed his memory nothing.

Owed his memory? What does that mean? This example seems to have been written by a person who knows little of grief. In all these months of steeping in the world of grief, I have not heard a single person mention owing the dead person's *memory* anything. Memories are all we have left and we treasure them, but we also know that memory is not a living creature to whom we must pay homage. We might feel obligations to those who are gone, obligations such as honoring their wishes as to funerals and disbursement of treasured possessions, but we fulfill those obligations out of love and because we find comfort and continuity in still being able to do things for our loved ones. But owing the memory we have of the person? Doesn't even make sense.

We bereft are all struggling to find a way to live with the hole in our lives, with the ongoing sadness, with the reality that grief is an unending (though perhaps diminishing) journey. No griever I have met has said, "Wait! I can't be happy. I owe too much to his memory." Grieving is a process, something we do, something that happens to us, but it is seldom the choice that is hinted at in the above example. Quite frankly, we are all sick of grieving, of being sad, but the only way not to be sad is to have our loved ones back with us, and since that is impossible in this world, we continue on as best as we can with our shattered lives. But we owe that to ourselves, not to his memory.

Day 251, Blog Post, **Grief: Loose Cannon on Deck**

A loose cannon conjures images of a weapon wildly

firing in all directions, but it actually refers to a cannon on the deck of a ship. Cannons needed to be lashed down, but in turbulent waters, cannons sometimes came loose and rolled around the deck. Their great weight (some weighed as much as 1800 lbs!) made those loose cannons a dangerous liability and they could crush a hapless sailor who got in the way.

That's exactly the way grief feels. Every time you feel as if you're getting a solid footing despite the turbulence of your new life . . . whack! That cannon comes loose and crushes you again.

It would be so much easier if the so-called stages of grief were actually stages that you can check off after you've experienced it. Denial. Check. Pain. Check. Anger. Check. Depression. Check. Acceptance. Check.

All done, right?

Wrong!

After you've gone through the list, there it comes again, the pain or the anger or the disbelief that he is gone, and you have to do it all over again. Add to that the innumerable stages that aren't commonly known such as isolation, anxiety, low self-esteem, confusion, panic, frustration, hopelessness, loneliness, bitterness, missing the person, fretfulness, hanging on, waiting for you know not what, and dozens of others. Not everyone who has experienced a significant loss goes through all the stages, but no matter what, we've all felt that loose cannon and wish we could just tie the dang thing up and get on with our lives.

So we do.

And then, comes another storm, there's that loose cannon again.

Can you sense the pettishness of my tone? Must be another stage I've never heard of. Well, check this one off, too.

Day 255, Blog Post, **Let It Be . . . Me**

You've probably seen the video (dozens of actors and actresses singing Paul McCartney's song, "Let It Be"). Almost everyone has. It's been emailed and remailed,

Facebooked and Twittered, blogged and Gathered, clogging cyberspace with the message: Let It Be. At first I thought that perhaps this was the answer to my confusion over the death of my mate of thirty-four years. Just go on with my life and let it be. Forget my grief. Forget the pain of losing him. Forget trying to make sense of it all. Just . . . let it be.

My second thought as I continued watching this very looooong and repetitive song (Sheesh! What was Paul McCartney thinking when he wrote it? Not much, apparently) was how my mate would have enjoyed seeing all those faces as they are today. We have so many of them in his movie collection, and they are always that age, the one they'd reached when they made that particular movie (such as a much younger Sherilyn Fenn in *The Don's Analyst* or a very young and fit Steve Guttenberg in *Surrender*).

My third thought was let what be what? And that's where the thoughts stalled—in a semantics word jam.

I finished watching the video, thinking nothing, just watching the parade of faces, but now I'm wondering if Let it Be is really a philosophy I want to embrace. It seems too accepting of life's vagaries and not enough of . . . well, embracing.

The whole purpose of going through grief is to process the pain and the loss, to mend your shattered life and heart so that one day you can embrace life in its entirety once again. I haven't dealt with all these months of tears, anger, frustration, emptiness, loneliness, pain, just to spend the rest of my life letting it be. I want to let it be me—the one who's strong enough not to have to simply let it be.

Day 262, Blog Post. **Letting it Be**

My previous post chronicled my thought processes as I watched the video "Let It Be" that is making the rounds. As I said in that bloggery, *At first I thought that perhaps this was the answer to my confusion over the death of my mate of thirty-four years. Just go on with my life and let it be. Forget my grief. Forget the pain of losing him. Forget trying to make sense of it all. Just . . . let it be.*

When I first wrote that a few days ago, something in me let loose, and though I claimed I did not want to let it be (whatever *it* is) I haven't been the same since. At least not exactly the same. I still had my usual Saturday upsurge of grief (preceded by a late night—I don't seem to be able to go to sleep until after 1:40 am on Friday night, the time of his death) but I felt sad rather than soul-broken. I've even had a few moments when I could actually feel glimmers of life.

I can't forget my grief or the pain of losing him, though both are slowly diminishing. And I can't stop trying to make sense of my life. That's who I am and always will be—a truth seeker. But I can let go of trying to make sense of his life.

It has haunted me all these months—the dual vision of the young radiant man he was when we met and the skin-covered skeleton he'd become. Were all those years of illness worth living? He was often in pain and wanted to be done with life, yet he kept striving to live until the very end. I remember those last years, months, days, and I still cry for him and his doomed efforts. But he doesn't need those tears. His ordeal only lives in my memory. And that is what I am letting be. It is not for me to make sense of his life or his death. It is not for me to keep suffering for him now that he is gone.

A fortune cookie I read the other day said, "Cleaning up the past will always clear up the future." Much of my grief has been about cleaning up the past—coming to terms with small every day betrayals, with dreams that never came true, with leftover worries. I have cleaned up the past, gradually worked through those conundrums. What is left is the habit of dwelling on the past, and that I can let be. It does neither of us any good.

Will it clear up the future for me? Perhaps. At the very least, it will help me face the future. Whatever that might be.

Day 264, **Grief Journal**
I've been dreaming about Jeff lately. He doesn't appear in the dreams, but I'm constantly searching for him.

Sometimes I catch a glimpse of someone who could be Jeff, but mostly I just search.

In my waking life, I've been keeping busy, not crying much, trying to get on with my life, trying to believe that it's a good thing I'm still alive, but what I'm really doing is pushing thoughts of him out of my mind. It's the only way I can find peace.

I had a strange thought the other day. I've been sorting through some of his movies, throwing out those I'll never watch again. (I'd like to keep them all, but I have too much stuff for someone who is rootless.) As I was putting one of the tapes in the VCR to check it out, I thought, "I hope he's really not coming back because he'd be furious to find out what I've done to his movie collection."

My life with Jeff is beginning to fade from me. My life is beginning to fade. So little of it feels real. What will my life be like a year from now? Ten years? Will things start mattering again? Who will I be? Still myself, of course. I don't seem to be able to get away from that core person.

Day 268, Blog Post, **The Gift of Possibilities**

I have been given a very special and unwelcome gift this year—the gift of possibilities.

Thirty-eight weeks ago my life mate—my soul mate—died. During the previous few years, the constraints of his illness bound our lives, and it felt as if we were doomed to an eternity of decreasing possibilities. Every day he became weaker, could do less, had fewer options. We could not plan for our future, knowing each day was all he might have. We could not even spend much time together—it took all his strength and concentration just to make it through another hour.

And so we lived. Waited.

His death brought enormous changes to my life, but during these months of grief, I have focused on the impossibilities. It is impossible for him to come back to me and it's impossible for me go home to him. It's impossible for us ever to have another conversation, watch a movie, play a game, take a trip, start over in a new location as we so often did during our decades together. It's impossible for me to stop missing him, impossible to conceive of living in a world from which he is absent. It's been impossible, too, to concede that perhaps my life could be easier without him. What difference does that make when our being together was all that ever mattered to me?

And yet, and yet . . .

I am getting glimmers of myself now, myself alone. I no longer have the financial and emotional burden of his illness. I am no longer weighted down by my own grief, though it is still a part of me, and probably always will be.

I still feel as if I am waiting, but I'm beginning to feel as if I'm waiting for something rather than simply waiting, though I don't know what I am waiting for. I do know that—slowly—the world of possibility is opening up to me again. I might not be able to do whatever I want—people are so wrong when they say anything is possible—but many things are probable when you've been given the gift of possibilities.

Day 274, **Dear Jeff,**

If you still exist in memory, then I took you for a walk last evening to show you the Christmas lights. You'd have enjoyed it—so many people around here have gone all out with decorations.

I cried most of the night. It was Friday night. And it being Christmas Eve didn't help. As usual, I couldn't go to bed until after 1:40 am. I watched movies, of course. That's what we always did during the holidays. One of the movies about killed me. Remember the Robert Urich movie where he runs by the house of a sad woman? She's taking care of her husband, who's been dying of a stroke for five years. It's funny how the movie meant one thing while I was on the bright side of grief's dividing line, and how it means something else from this side.

She found letters from her husband after he died. I wish I had letters from you, something I could read that would sound as if you were talking to me. But everything talks to me—our household goods, the research notes you took, your perpetual calendar and other mementoes. And your movies, of course. You taped each of them for a reason—sometimes I feel as if you taped them for me, to help me get through this grief.

Second chances is a theme in the Urich movie, as in so many of your movies. We both wanted a second chance at the life we'd hoped for, and I have a second chance— perhaps—to create a life for myself, but I wanted the second chance for *us*. It's easier in many ways not having anyone but myself to consider, but I'd rather have a second chance with you. I'd like us to start over somewhere nice, have fun.

How could it have come to this, Jeff? You dead, me in this limbo? Why couldn't we be together today, watching movies, a feast spread out around us? For some reason, while I'm writing this, I feel as if I really am writing to you. You seem very real to me, as if it's been just a few weeks since we were together rather than months.

I think of you often, but I don't call out for you as much as I used to, perhaps because I haven't been wandering in the desert lately—it's been raining most of the week. I still yearn for you. It's like an itch, a hunger, or a need deep inside magnified beyond bearing.

I love you, Jeff. I hope you had a good Christmas.

Day 275, Blog Post, **I Am a Nine-Month Grief Survivor**

Thirty-four years ago, I walked into a health food store, and my world was never the same. It wasn't love at first sight, this first time I saw the man with whom I would share more than three decades of my life. It was a primal recognition. Something deep inside me, something beneath consciousness, wailed, "But I don't even like men with blond hair and brown eyes."

I had no expectation of ever spending my life with this radiantly wise and intelligent man. It was enough to know he was alive. The world, which had seemed so inhospitable, became a place of hope and possibilities simply because he lived. Over the months our connection grew, and gradually our lives became entwined.

It confused us at times, our connection. Neither of us were particularly romantic, and we didn't bring each other fairy-tale happiness. But we were together, and in the end, as at the beginning, being together was all that mattered.

But we aren't together any more. Nine months ago, he died. And my world will never be the same.

I am doing okay—can even go for a week or two at a time without a major grief attack—but I still feel as if parts of me are missing. Grief shattered me, and I've put the pieces back together as best as I can despite those missing pieces. I now get glimpses of hope, of possibilities, of building a new life for myself. I know there will be times of overwhelming grief and times of peace, times of sorrow and times of gladness. But he isn't here to share those times. That I cannot comprehend.

Until I became one of the bereft, I thought grief was self-centered and self-pitying, and there is some truth to that. I do feel sorry for myself at times, but mostly I struggle to comprehend the meaning of our connected lives, his dying, and my continued life. I struggle to accept that while (perhaps) there is a second chance of happiness for me in this life, there is none for him. I struggle to understand his goneness. Sometimes the need to go home to him over-whelms me, and I have to learn—again—that his being gone from this life means I can never go home. He was my home. Someday I might learn to find "home" within myself, but until then, I am adrift in a world that once again feels inhospitable.

During those first days and weeks of struggling to survive grief, I kept screaming to myself, "I can't do this." I still feel like screaming those words occasionally, but I have learned that yes, I can survive this, because I have. And I will continue to survive.

Tenth Month

Day 281, Blog Post, **Building Hopes and Creating Dreams (New Years Day)**
And so ends the worst year of my life.

Last year was a time of soul-shattering loss, grief, and strange blessings. It was a time of despair and self-realization, transition and adjustment. But of course, you know all that—I've made no secret of my ordeal, chronicling every painful stage of my journey. Many people endure worse traumas than the death of a soul mate, and they continue living without whimpering, which has made me feel a bit self-indulgent and whiny with my grief bloggeries, yet that was never my intention. The impact of grief after a major loss seems to be one more thing that has been discounted in our discount culture, and I simply wanted to tell the truth.

Oddly, I still don't know the truth of it. It seems unreal at times. Was I really that woman? That woman who watched a man slowly die, who wanted the suffering to end, yet whose love was so ineffectual she couldn't make him well or take away a single moment of his pain? That woman so connected to another human being she still feels broken nine months after his death? That woman who screamed the pain of her loss to the winds?

I've always considered myself a passionless woman, so how can that woman be me? During periods when I don't feel the weight of his absence (I never feel his presence, though sometimes his absence feels normal, as if he's simply in another room), during periods of emotional calm, my stoic side rules, making my grief feel fake, as if it's something I'm doing to make myself seem important. Yet other times the desperate need to go home to him, to see him one more time, claws at me, tearing me apart.

Making the situation even more unreal, I can barely remember what he looked like—I do not think in images, so

121

it's understandable (though distressing) that I have no clear image of him in my mind. Even worse, I don't have a photo that matches what I remember of him. (The only one I have was taken fifteen years ago.)

Nor do I have a clear sense of time. Sometimes it feels as if he died just a couple of months ago. Sometimes it feels like years. The demarcation between our shared life and my solitary life was once so stark it was like the edge of a cliff. All I could see was the past and what I had lost. The living I have done in the past nine months has blurred that edge, adding to the sense of unreality.

I have learned much this year. I learned the importance of importance. If there is nothing of importance in your life, you have to find something and make it important. I learned the importance of goals, even if it's only the goal of getting through one more day. I learned the importance of hope, though hope for what I still don't know, but that is part of the journey—building hopes, creating dreams, finding reasons to live.

And so begins a new calendar year.

Day 284, Blog Post, **New Year, New Beginning?**

I've never put emphasis on the start of a new year because it's a relatively arbitrary date. The calendar numbers change, but that's all. It's not a universal new beginning. The Chinese New Year this year is on February 3, the Jewish New Year is on September 28, and various communities in the Hindu religion have different dates—January 15, March 22, April 14, April 15, August 17, October 27. January 1 is not even the beginning of a new seasonal cycle. Nor is there any personal demarcation—no black line separates the old from the new. You carry the old year with you because you have the same problems, sadnesses, hopes, fears. In other words, you are still you.

There is a newness to January 1, though, and that is the newness of a new day. Unlike the year, each day is a new beginning. You wake up, and for a second everything is untouched—like new fallen snow—and you almost believe you can be anyone you want to be, do anything you want to do. Then the truth hits you.

Still, there's hope, so I make daily resolutions instead of yearly ones. I have a list of a dozen do's and don'ts that I would follow in a perfect world. I'm lucky to do about half of them each day, but it varies. Two days ago I did only a couple. Yesterday I did all but two. Today, of course, I resolve to follow everything on my list. The list includes such things as weight lifting and stretching, walking, writing, blogging, promoting, eating a big salad, drinking lots of water, staying away from sugar and wheat. As I said, in a perfect world . . .

Despite that, I did toast the coming year, more as a symbol of newness than the reality of it. I've learned that since nothing seems important any more, I have to make something important every day. And toasting a new year seemed as good as anything to importantize. (Yeah, I know—there's no such word as importantize, but just for today—this new day— there is.)

Day 285, **Dear Jeff,**

I haven't been getting much sleep lately. I don't want to go to bed, and I wake too early. This morning when I awoke, I felt angry at you for putting me through all this agony. I shouldn't be angry. None of this is your fault. I have a hunch the anger is a part of letting go. I don't want to let go—you know that. If possible, I'd do whatever was necessary to get us back together. But . . . and this is a big but . . . you are beyond my reach. If I demonize you or belittle our relationship, the grief is easier to handle, but I won't do that. It's important to deal with the truth—the good and the bad— and the truth is I still cannot bear that you are gone. Silly, isn't it? I must be doing better, though, to let the anger through since I so seldom get angry, but the anger didn't last long. It was just a brief fizz.

I told a minister friend that I knew for a fact my love had no healing powers, and he said, "What makes you think death isn't a form of healing?" Hmm. That sure gave me something to ponder!

Things are changing in my life. People I was once close to, I no longer have much connection with. Because of it, I'm becoming more of a hermit than I'd planned. I wish I knew what I want to do or where I want to go. I'm waiting, I guess, to see where life throws me next.

No matter what I do in the future, no matter who I do it with, you do know it isn't a betrayal of you or our life together? I need to find a way to get through the coming years without you, though how I'm supposed to do that, I don't know. Well, yes, I do—one day at a time. Adios, compadre. I love you.

Day 286, Blog Post, **Grief: The Great Yearning**

Now that my grief for my lost soul mate is evolving away from a focus on all I've lost and the accompanying pain, I can see the process more clearly. Perhaps for some people the stages of grief—denial, guilt, anger, depression, acceptance—hold true, but for me and for most of the bereft I have met on this journey, those stages have little meaning. For most of us, anger and even guilt are more like quickly passing moods than lingering phases. Some of us get depressed, but most of us don't. We just get damn sad, which is not the same thing as depression. I've been in that dark pit and I know what it's like. This sorrow, no matter how intense, is not depression. And acceptance is not the end—in itself acceptance brings no peace. What does bring peace is feeling the grief and letting it evolve into something we can live with because the loss—the yearning—will always be a part of us. Getting to that point can take years, depending on the depth of the relationship.

Grief is an incredibly complex state that constantly changes and constantly brings changes. The underlying emotion of grief is yearning, not guilt or anger. Even after we've put our shattered psyches back together as best as we can, even after we've come to an acceptance of our new situation, the yearning to see our beloved one last time can be overwhelmingly painful. The yearning (such a mild word for the ache or craving or hunger that tears at us) is often manageable, other times it shoots through us like a geyser bursting out of calm waters. Even decades after losing a spouse, or so I've been told, we bereft still feel the loss, still yearn for our mates.

A friend who lost her life mate four months after I lost mine, told me how much she hates people telling her to "move on". She's not like me, spouting her pain into cyberspace for all to see. If you didn't know she'd experienced such a soul-shattering loss, you'd never be able to guess it—she's keeping her grief to herself lest it burden others. She's taking care of her family. She's accepting the responsibility for an aging parent. She made the holidays special for those around her. She's writing. She's even going out and having fun, or at least as much as is possible considering her situation. In fact, she's doing all that she ever did, and doing it well. Yet people tell her to move on with her life. What else is there to move on to? Her grief in no way debilitates her. It's simply a part of her life, this ache to see her mate one more time.

Searching is another major component of grief that is ignored in the "stages" concept. We bereft search for our mates in crowds. We cry out for them, especially at the beginning. We search for them in our dreams. Of course we know we won't find them. This isn't a mental aberration, and it certainly isn't denial. It's simply a way of coping with the unthinkable. How can our loved ones be gone so completely? It's the goneness that confuses us, pains us. It destroys everything we always accepted about the world. (Of course we knew all lives end in death, but we didn't KNOW it.) As the search for our lost one diminishes, we begin searching for ourselves, for our place in this new, unthinkable world.

It would be so much easier to deal with grief if we had a list of stages to go through and to check off as we experience them, but that simply isn't the case.

So we yearn, and we search, and we go on living.

Day 287, **Dear Jeff,**

I don't seem to want to get out of bed today. I'm not depressed, just empty. I'm in a grief hiatus, feeling calm, but not knowing what to think about anything. I savor these grief-less times. They make me realize I can go on alone. We shared so much that even as I get to where I can accept the situation, even accept that I might find happiness, I can't forget that it's at your expense. I wonder what this feels like from your perspective. I know you want me to go on, to get what I can from life—you told me that—but still, where are you in all this? At some point our separation has to be complete, doesn't it? I have to realize that whatever I say or think or do has no affect on you—it can't change anything that happened. It can't bring you back.

Remember Iron Sam in *Daughter Am I* telling Mary that a person experiences death only once? Well, you were my experience of death. The utter undoableness of it—the finality—shocked me to my core. I think that shock is what can only be experienced once. A prognosis of my own death probably won't have the same impact. Will I have your strength, your courage? I won't have you, and that might not be a bad thing. Maybe my death will be easier to handle if I know I'm not going to devastate anyone when I go.

People always talk about finding someone to grow old with, but I'm not sure that's a blessing. Lately, I've been seeing a lot of very old couples (this area is filled with hospitals, doctors offices, oncology clinics, pain treatment centers, nursing homes) and I try to imagine what it would be like for the two of us to deal with each other's old age infirmities. I'm glad you'll be spared that. It was hard enough for you to die without having to worry about my dying, too.

There's a chance I will live for a long time, and there's a chance I will forget you, but part of me will always remember. I wish you were waiting for me on the other side of grief so we could start a new life together, and in a way you will be there—you are still so much a part of me. Maybe literally a part of me. If we're all made of stardust, if everything is commingled, how much more commingled are we who spent so many decades in each other's company! Then there are all the movies we watched together, the books we shared, the thousand upon thousand of hours of electric conversation, the ideas we developed, the businesses we created—all those are part of me.

One thing this experience has taught me is to bear unbearable emotional trauma. Some experiences need to be lived whole, without chipping away at the rough angles or looking for a bright side to make them more bearable. Grief is one of those experiences. Even though I never figured out how to survive my grief, I've come through the worst of it.

I don't suppose the future will be easy, but it might be easier than I expect. I'm much stronger than I thought I was—these past months have taught me that—and I know I can bear almost anything. I've already lived through the worst year (and the worst day) of my life. I've come to terms with so much that is unthinkable and unknowable, such as the sheer finality of your being gone, that I'm more willing to take things as they come. Of course, I'll still try to make sense of the senseless, but that is my nature.

This sounds like good-bye, doesn't it? But it isn't. I'm sure the geyser of grief will send up more jets of pain, and I'll write to you again, but this does seem to be the end of something. Maybe grief as a gestation period? It has been a little over nine months since you've been gone, maybe I'm being reborn into a new life.

Are you glad you lived your life with me? Sometimes I got the impression you were as helpless as I was to break our connection. We never did understand it. Was it real? Eternal? Or simply two pieces of a puzzle that fit together? Will we ever know? Not that it matters if we don't—the connection is broken now. And I'm free to do . . . what? I don't know. It might take me the rest of my life to find out.

I hope you know how much I loved you, and love you still. Adios, compadre. Be at peace. I will be okay.

Day 288, **Grief Journal**

Saturday, again. I stayed in bed all morning reading because I did not want to get up and face another Saturday. Friday nights and Saturdays continue to be difficult. I watched movies last night until my private witching hour of 1:40am.

The longer Jeff is gone, the more I see what I've lost. When we were together, everything was normal, so I couldn't see how extraordinary our lives were. We created all our own recipes and fixed all our own meals, built our own business, spent years researching the mysteries of the world. And we had such wonderful marathon talks that lasted for days. We didn't try to convince the other of our position—we each brought truth and thought to the conversation, and together we created a greater reality. There was no reason to argue—it was never about his opinion versus mine. It was about the truth—the truth as far as we could reconstruct it together.

A woman who lost her mate four months after I lost Jeff asked me the other day if I loved Jeff more now than when he was alive, and in a way I do. The problems of his growing ill health got in the way the last few years, clouding my vision of him. Now that those problems and my reaction to them are no longer a factor, I can see the truth of him again (or at least more of the truth than I did) and the love shines through.

Grief comes and goes, but love stays. And grows.

Day 296, Blog Post, **Grief Update: Throwing a Tantrum**

I haven't blogged about grief recently. Actually, I haven't blogged about anything for a while. I'm in a transitional stage—not sure what I'm feeling, not sure what direction I want to go with this blog, not sure what I want to do with the rest of my life. I've been purposely thinking of other things than the death of my soul mate, though grief does geyser up without my volition now and again, especially on Saturdays, the day of the week he died. Even if I'm not consciously aware of that day, still, nine and a half months later, something in me acknowledges the date, and sadness grabs hold of me.

Except not this Saturday. This Saturday (yesterday), I wanted to throw myself on the ground and beat the floor in a full-fledged tantrum. I've never thrown a tantrum in my life, but if I'd been someplace where no one could hear me, I would have made an exception. I wanted desperately to talk to him. His death was the most significant aspect of our lives since the day we met, and he's not here for us to compare notes. I want to know how he's doing. I want to know *what* he's doing. Is he doing anything, feeling anything? Or is he drifting on a sea of light, like a newborn star?

It seems impossible that he's gone, and the simple truth is that I don't want him to be dead. Sure, I can handle it. Sure, I can deal with living the rest of my life alone. Sure, I can do whatever I need to do. But I don't want to. I want him. I want to see him. I want to see his smile. I want . . . I want . . . I want . . . All those wants erupted Saturday night, hence the desire to throw a tantrum.

I've never heard of tantrum as a phase of grief, but I've never heard of most of the stages I've gone through. My grief cycle does not at all resemble the stages defined by Kübler-Ross. Hers is a simplistic view of grief when in fact grief is a cyclical emotional and physical quagmire. The frequency of my grief eruptions has diminished, and so has the worst of my pain, but the hole his death created in my life remains. I try filling the emptiness with physical activity, talking to people, reading, writing, even eating, but nothing fills the want.

How can someone who was so much a part of my life be gone? Even if he is waiting for me on the other side of eternity, he's still gone from this life. And I don't want him to be. I want . . . I want . . . I want . . .

Clear the area. I feel a tantrum coming on

Day 303, Blog Post, **Trying to Relight My Life**
When I was in high school, I participated in a thesis project for a doctoral candidate. He was trying to prove (I

think) that given the right tools, anyone could teach and anyone could learn. The high school students were to teach kids from the lower grades about various aspects of science. During the first class, I handed each of my students a battery and a light bulb and asked them to turn on the light. They couldn't of course. I asked what they needed, and one kid said they needed a wire. I handed everyone a wire. A bit of experimentation later, they realized they needed a second wire. So, I handed out another wire, and in a very short time all those light bulbs were lit.

I've been thinking a lot about that recently—not the program so much as those wires linking the battery terminals to the light bulb. It seems to me that ever since the death of my life mate, one of the wires is missing from my electrical system, and nothing lights me.

Take movies, for example.

My family didn't have a television when I was growing up, and we seldom went to the movies, so I read to get my daily dose of stories. I wasn't a speed reader, but was a skimmer—if there was a boring part, such as long descriptions, inane dialogue, and action scenes that went nowhere, I fast forwarded. Skimmed in other words. As a young adult, I went to the movies occasionally, but found most of them dull since I couldn't skip over the boring parts.

After we'd been together for a few years, my life mate and I signed up for an assortment of movie channels. Back then there were only four premium channels, and those channels offered dozens and dozens of new choices every month. The two of us became entranced with movies. It was something we could share, and the enjoyment we each felt enhanced the enjoyment the other felt. The humor was funnier when shared. The tender scenes more touching. The scary scenes more horrifying. And I wasn't bored. Didn't need to skim.

He started taping the movies we liked, then he taped those he liked that I didn't (such as genre westerns and war movies) then he went on to tape good parts of bad movies and finally he taped the best of the rest.

He's gone now, but his movie collection remains. I have over 1000 movies to sort through (since I won't be able to keep them all), so I've been watching a lot of movies lately, and I discovered something interesting. The movies that thrilled us, made us laugh, electrified us, the movies that radiated life—the movies that once seemed life personified—are now simply . . . movies. Films. Faded stories on a flat screen. As with the films I saw as a young adult (before I met him), these movies now seem to have nothing to do with me. I watch them. Can even enjoy them, but that's all. Turns out, I needed two "wires" to make the stories live in me, and one of the wires is permanently defunct.

I'm not even attempting to watch the movies we especially loved, the ones that seemed to be made just for us. Without the other electrical "wire" these movies might also prove to be lifeless streams of motion, which would be unbearably sad. And if the movies still hold up, I couldn't bear the sadness of watching them alone, without him. I'm sure eventually I'll find the courage to view them again, but not today.

If the missing wire only affected movie watching, I'd chalk it up to one more loss among so many, but the truth is, with his being gone, nothing seems real. It was as if his smile when I told him good news or his commiseration at bad news or his laugh at silly news grounded me, and made everything more vibrant.

I am getting back into the swing of my life, and I'm starting to feel "normal." Perhaps someday I might even find a way to relight my life despite that missing wire.

Day 306, **Dear Jeff,**

Tomorrow it will be ten months since I saw you last. I don't know how I survived all these months, but here I am. The main problem right now is a great yearning for you. The want/need to talk to you is overwhelming at times.

I hadn't been going to the grief group—I didn't want to talk about you or my grief any more—but I'm going to start going again. I've noticed that every time I make plans for something special, such as my upcoming trip to St. Simons Island to speak at a writers' conference, I have an upsurge of grief. I feel like such a child, wanting what I cannot have. You'd think by now I would have accepted that I'll never see you again and just deal with it. Actually, I have accepted that I'll never see you again. I know you're dead. I just don't want you to be. And every time I plan something new, it's like I have to rearrange my mental furniture to accommodate your absence.

There is still so much to grieve for. Sometimes I grieve for that young man I met at the health food store, and that is the saddest part because I know what became of him. I know his dreams that didn't come true, the way he struggled to deal with the impossible hand he'd been dealt, the heart-breaking way he died.

Shortly after we met, I heard that Firefall song, "You are the Woman That I've Always Dreamed of." I thought they were singing "You are the one that I've always dreamed of," and that's the way I felt. From the start, I really did know you were the one. I still remember the way you looked at me the first time we hugged. Such a radiant smile!

Well, you're still in my heart, my mind, my soul. I don't know how to get you out. I don't know if I want to. I want the impossible—you. Silly, huh?

Day 307, Blog Post, **I Am a Ten-Month Grief Survivor**
I mentioned to someone the other day that it's been ten weeks since the death of my life mate and that I didn't know how I managed to survive that long, then it hit me. It hasn't been ten weeks. It's been ten *months.* How is it possible to live almost a year with half your heart ripped out? I still don't know, but I do the only thing I can: live.

After the nine-month mark, I had a respite from grief. I liked the symmetry of nine months of grief (gestation) before being born into a new life, but as happens with grief, the respite was merely that—a respite. A couple of weeks ago, the need to see my mate one more time grew so great it felt as if the yearning would explode from my body like the creature in *Alien*. The feeling came and went for a while, and now the creature has gone back into hibernation. But still, the yearning lingers.

I'm learning to live with the remnants of my grief. From others who have also borne such a loss, I've come to understand this is the next phase of grief—not soul-destroying pain as at the beginning, but blips of varying intensity and frequency. I know I can deal with this new stage of grief because I have been dealing with my grief all along, but still, a part of me rebels at the necessity.

Planning signifies hope and is supposed to be a sign of healing. Strangely (or perhaps not strangely; perhaps it's to be expected) every time I make plans, I have an upsurge of grief. Plans take me further away from him and our life. They remind me of similar things we did together, and they tell me that from now on, he won't be sharing new experiences with me. Still, I am not holding myself back. I need to fill the hole he left behind, and new experiences are one way of doing that.

In the past four months I've gone to various art galleries. I've seen Mesoamerican antiquities, aristocratic clothing through the ages, local artists, classic art work. I went to a wild life sanctuary where they take care of captive-bred animals that zoos don't want. I went to the beach. In May, I'll be going to The Scribbler's Retreat Writers' Conference where I'll be a speaker.

All this shows that I'm moving on, and yet . . .

And yet he's still gone. That goneness is something I struggle with—how can he be dead? I wanted his suffering to be over, so I was relieved when he died, but somehow I never understood how very gone he would be. I don't want him to be gone, but he's not coming back, and there is not a damn thing I can do about it.

Eleventh Month

Day 313, Blog Post, **Advice to the Newly Bereft**

A couple of newly bereft joined the grief group I go to, and seeing how lost and bewildered they are showed me how far I have come these past months. I've reached a modicum of peace (though I still have moments of intense grief) and I don't feel quite so lost and bewildered.

The Kübler-Ross formula for grief is so ingrained in all of us that we think those are the only stages of grief, but I have discovered dozens of phases more universal and potent than denial, guilt, anger, depression. Loss and bewilderment are two such phases. They are major components of grief, though I haven't found them listed anywhere as a stage the bereft have to deal with.

The worst problem of grief, of course, is that someone who was a vital part of our life is dead. The second worst problem is that we are flooded with so many emotions, topped off with excruciating pain, that it is almost impossible to sort everything out. All these emotions gridlock the brain's synapses, and we are left feeling lost and alone and totally bewildered. Where did our loved one go? How can he no longer be here? How can the world continue without his presence? How can we continue without his support and love? How can he be so very gone?

That "loss" everyone tells us they are sorry for is not our loved ones. Our loved ones are not lost, not misplaced; they are dead. We bereft are the ones who are lost. Whatever place we thought we had in the world is gone, perhaps forever. The world is different without our loved ones, and this is especially so if the dead we loved was a life partner, a soul mate. They'd become such a part of the fabric of our lives, of our very being, that when death rips them from us, we no longer recognize ourselves. We wander lost, bewildered, in this alien world. Some people manage to find themselves again, others become so changed they never find their way back.

I'd gone through the typical stages of grief before my life mate—my soul mate—died. I'd denied, raged, bargained, accepted, so that I thought I was "over" him, that after his death, my life would continue, sadder, but not much different. The depth of my grief, my loss, my pain, my bewilderment stunned me. I'd gone through all the stages of grief, so I should be okay, right? Wrong. Real grief begins where those so-called stages of grief leave off. Those stages of grief were first noted as the way people learned to accept their coming death, and they bear only a shadow of a resemblance to what those left behind experience.

My life mate and I used to talk about who had it worse—I thought he had it worse because he was the one suffering. He thought I had it worse. It turns out he was right. His suffering is over, but mine will last the rest of my life. My grief will continue to change, to go through additional changes, will abate, might even be forgotten at times, but it is now a part of my life.

And he is not.

That is the crux of the issue, the cause of all that bewilderment, pain, and loss. How do you live with someone who is no longer there? How do you live without them? Here's how: you find comfort wherever you can, however you can. (Besides drink and recreational drugs, that is.) No matter what you do to get through the worst of your pain, no matter how crazy it is, be assured that others have done it, too. Hug the urn with his ashes, carry his identification, smell or cuddle or wear his clothes, talk to him, scream for him, cover the wall with his photos, write to him, write blogs about your grief. Do whatever it takes to get you through, because, as hard as it is to accept, you are still alive.

Day 318, **Dear Jeff,**

It hit me last night that you're really gone, that you exist only in me now, and it was like losing you all over again. I've been trying to believe that you still exist in some form, but that attempt has failed. I do so wish you were living happily by some cosmic lake, being lulled by peaceful waters and gentle breezes, a cat asleep in your lap, but that is such a fantasy it dissolves before I can grasp hold of it.

I can't do this, Jeff. I'm tired of the resurgences of grief, tired of your being gone, tired of the world feeling so wrong. I still don't see the point of living without you. You satisfied something in me, supplied a piece of life's puzzle, and you took the piece with you when you died. Just one more thing I will have to learn to supply for myself.

I'm more at peace than I've been, more accepting of the idea of your death, but I will never accept your death itself. I can go for days without shedding a tear, but sometimes, like this morning, grief doubles me over with such pain that I can't help weeping.

Today is the anniversary of the day we talked about courage. It was the last of our marathon talks—we talked all day, said everything we had to say, and we felt close to each other. How can that talk have been a year ago? I see us clearly, you in bed, holding still so as not to aggravate the pain, me sitting by your side.

It's a constant in my life, this yearning to talk with you, see you smile, be with you. I keep wanting to apologize for whatever I did that was so terrible you had to leave me, though I know there wasn't anything. I keep listening for the phone, hoping you'll call and tell me all is forgiven and I can come home. How can this be so hard? Why can't I understand?

I'm trying to be courageous. I love you, Jeff. I hope you are at peace.

Day 319, **Dear Jeff,**

I can't sleep and am too tired to get up and do anything. If you were here, you'd be up, fixing your morning protein drink, doing your exercises, filtering the drinking water for the day. I woke to those sounds for decades and didn't realize until just now how they formed the sound track of my life.

I still feel as if this is our life. Ironically, I feel that most strongly when I am not thinking about you, when I feel "normal," as if you're here, perhaps in another room. If I think about you, I remember you're gone, and the grief comes. (I'm not yet to the point where thinking about you brings me comfort and smiles.) The wanting—the yearning—whether acknowledged with tears or not, is always a part of me.

I've been sorting through more of your movies. Sometimes I feel guilty for getting rid of the ones I don't like. Other times, when I get a blip of anger at your being gone, I find satisfaction in throwing them away.

Ah, Jeff, look what's happened to us. I wish I could put my arms around you and keep you safe. Take care of yourself.

Day 320, **Grief Journal**

During the first months after Jeff died, I sometimes felt as if I weren't handing my grief well. I cried around others at the beginning (couldn't talk about his death without tears streaming down my face) but later I did my grieving in private. Only I knew what I was doing to assuage my grief, so why would I think I wasn't handling it well? Because I was weeping and wailing. In our present culture, tears are considered to be a sign of weakness, but who decided that weeping and wailing are inappropriate ways of relieving the incredible stress, pain, and angst of losing a long time mate? Such releases are necessary. Otherwise, where does the pain go? Either it stays inside to cause emotional and physical damage, or it gets relieved by truly inappropriate behavior such as misplaced anger and hatred.

Through thousands of movies and books, we are taught to be stoic, to hold back our tears, to be cool. Yul Brynner in *The Magnificent Seven* was the epitome of western cool, gliding across the film's landscape without a single show of emotion. Cinematic heroes such as he could relieve their tensions and emotions through shooting rampages, hard liquor, and harder women. Perhaps, if these men had wept, the west (at least the mythological west) would have been a more genteel place.

Many people, when hit with the maelstrom of emotions called grief, feel as if they are going crazy. Oddly, I didn't, even though some of my actions and reactions would have made me a suitable candidate for a fictional madwoman. (Makes me wonder. Were those women hidden away in attics and tower rooms really crazy, or were they simply grief-stricken?) I knew I was sane, knew I was well adjusted, so any emotions I felt or things I did to comfort myself, by definition, were normal. Not having to worry about being crazy enabled me to deal with the pain itself rather than my reaction to it.

I do not know how I recognized the importance of tears, of feeling the pain now so that later it doesn't take over my life, but I understood it from the beginning. And since I am afraid of pain, I do not know where I got the courage to embrace the agony of losing Jeff, to face it head on, arms open wide. But I did, and I still do. I will learn to manage my grief—I am learning—and that means crying when the need arises. I don't cry where anyone can see me, mostly because my tears are private but also because I don't want to make people feel bad since there is nothing they can do about my sorrow.

And that, perhaps, is the real reason for tears being frowned on in our culture. We don't want to be confronted with the outward show of someone's grief because it forces us to confront our own weakness in the face of life's (and death's) enormity.

Can't say as I blame people for shying away from the subject. I sure wish I didn't have to confront the enormity of death, but with Jeff gone, I really have no choice.

Day 324, **Dear Jeff,**

Can I come home? Please? Whatever I did, I promise I won't do it again.

I keep thinking ten and a half months is long enough to have gotten on with my life, but it isn't. It's barely a nick in time. And I am getting on with my life. At the grief group the other day, they gave us a paper listing the ways you know you're dealing with the loss—such as being able to drive alone without crying, being able to concentrate to read, making plans for the future—and most of the things on the list I've been doing from the beginning. What I can't deal with is that terrible need to go home. Home to you.

I came across a saying the other day, "time has a way of weeding out the trivial." My grief isn't getting weeded out. And it sure as hell isn't trivial. I keep thinking if I can come home, I won't need to feel this way any more. I keep wanting to go back, to put my arms around you, hold on to you so you can't leave. But you didn't leave. You died. And I sure couldn't protect you from that.

I'm trying new things, making new friends, but nothing fills the hole you left behind.

Adios, compadre. I love you.

Day 325, Blog Post, **The First Terrible Anniversaries of Grief**

The first anniversaries, holidays, and special days after a loved one's death are difficult because we are so intensely aware that the person is no longer here to share in the joyous occasions. This is especially true if that person is a spouse, a life mate, a soul mate. Whatever traditions we developed together become obsolete when only one of us remains to carry on. The pain, the yearning to be together once more can be devastating on these days.

If those first anniversaries do not mark joyous occasions and celebrations but days of horror, the pain is oh, so much worse.

This has been a particularly difficult month for many who lost their mates because Valentine's Day is shoved down our throats. Wherever we go, we see images of happy couples. We remember we once were loved, once were part of a couple, and now we are not. Oddly enough, my upsurge in grief this month has nothing to do with Valentine's Day. We were not a romantic couple, did not see the point of following the crowd and celebrating a day just because someone once decided we should. We ignored the day, hence it has no baggage to bring me pain. In fact, today was a good day for me—I had lunch with a couple of friends from my grief group. We have graduated from the need for the group but still need the companionship of those who have experienced the same losses, so today we initiated our own little social group. There was no maudlin talk, just the normal pleasantries of friends sharing a meal.

Still, this has been a dreadful month for me, a month of painful anniversaries. A year ago last week, my life mate—my soul mate—bent down to pick up something off the floor and pain hit him so severely, it sent him to bed for the rest of his life. A year ago next week we got the diagnosis. At the beginning of March, when he saw a doctor for the last time, the oncologist told him he had three to six months to live. Two days after that, we signed up for hospice. Three weeks later, he died.

I hadn't thought of these days as anniversaries, so I did not steal myself for the onrush of grief. But grief has a schedule all its own, and it came for me. Again. How can his descent into these final stages of dying have begun a year ago? Those days seem so close that if my arms were long enough, I could reach behind me and touch him. Hug him. Keep him safe.

Today, thinking about his last weeks of unendurable pain, I feel self-indulgent for all my yearning to have him back. How could I ever subject him to that again? And yet, like a child, I weep for what I cannot have. I wonder what, in my youth or childhood, I did that was so terrible to deserve such punishment. I listen for the phone, hoping he'll call me and tell me he forgives me and I can come home.

Grief is irrational. It stems from a part of us that has no logic. I know I did nothing to send him away. I know he is never going to call me again. I know I am not being punished for some long ago transgression.

And yet the grief keeps pounding at me during this time of terrible anniversaries.

Day 328, **Dear Jeff,**

I am so damn tired of your being dead. I got tired of your being sick all the time (though nowhere near as tired of it as you were) but now I'm even more tired of your being gone. I thought as time passed it would get easier, but it gets harder because the longer you're gone, the more the need to see you builds. And builds.

Sometimes I'm resigned to our situation, knowing there's not a single thing either of us can do about it, other times bleakness engulfs me. I was so wrong about grief—it's not the self-indulgent, self-pitying emotion I presumed it was. It's physical. Part of me is gone. Amputated. Was that part you? Something you fulfilled in me? A feeling of rightness that we were together?

I know I have to find a way of filling the roles you played in my life, either in myself or from others, but too many of the roles were unique to us—or if not unique, rare—something we created between us. I can find companionship and conversation, but I will never find the sort of electric energy that crackled between us when we went on one of our conversational excursions from history to music to movies to philosophy to books to science and back again to history. I'll never find someone I can say anything to, someone who won't filter my words through his of her own prejudices, opinions, and emotions the way I could with you. I'll never find anyone else who can talk dispassionately and intelligently about passionate subjects.

I'm not sure I'll ever be able to find anyone to fulfill the role of "home." I should be able to find it within me because now that you're gone, wherever I am is home, but there is more to home than a place or a person or a feeling. It's about being able to be who we are, to live in an environment where we can transcend who we are, to be free to experiment with new ideas, new ways of being/thinking, knowing someone will be there to catch us if we fall.

I hate this, Jeff. How am I supposed to live all the coming years missing you? Maybe the best I can hope for is to do what I'm doing—living despite my missing you.

Day 330, **Dear Jeff,**

I keep waiting to get over your death, but there is no getting over it because no matter what happens or how I feel, you're still dead. I know there will come a time when my grief isn't so raw (sheesh—ten and a half months of grief should have given me emotional calluses, but they haven't). The need to see you one more time is so overwhelming at times that I cannot bear it. I was always a pragmatist, but there is no way to be pragmatic about this. I hate what life did to you. You deserved so much more than you got. You were a good man, kinder and smarter than you ever knew.

I had to take a break to pound the pillows.

I wish I could go back to your last days at home and hold you, keep you safe

Adios, compadre. Be safe.

Day 334, Blog Post, **Surprised by Grief**

I continue to be surprised by the intensity and depth and variability of grief. It's been more than ten months since my life mate—my soul mate—died. Most days now I feel normal, but "normal" for me is his being safe at home, perhaps in the other room, perhaps outside shoveling snow or watering our trees. The renewed realization that he is gone from this life still brings me raw pain. I'm getting used to being alone—in some ways, that aloneness feels normal, too. Until I met him, I'd always expected to be alone, and so part of me is looping back to that earlier life when I had only my concerns to worry about.

Still, despite that normalcy, there are days when it feels as if he just left, as if he walked out on me (or I walked out on him) and it's a matter of time until we reconcile our differences. I don't know where such thoughts come from— we had no major differences. Well, except for the soul-shaking differences that came when our journeys diverged— his into death, mine into continued life.

I mentioned before that love and grief were the bookends of a relationship. Because of its intensity, the ability to change a person's life and outlook, and the all-consuming focus on another person, grief seems to mimic falling in love, though in a bleaker, blacker, lonelier way. And like love, grief stirs up your depths, making you realize you are more than you ever thought you could be. As I'm slowly beginning to define my life solely by me, not by "us", I'm seeing another similarity. When a couple embarks on a life together, they learn to depend on each other, to find ways to complement each other, to meld their likes and dislikes, their hopes and frustrations into a workable emotional environment for both parties. When half of a couple dies, the person left behind has to find a way to unmeld. To go from thinking about both of you, to thinking solely of yourself, to depending solely on yourself. It's hard and painful and feels futile at times. (Because, you think, if life is worth living, he would still be here.)

It's like a teeter-totter. When one person leaves abruptly, you crash to the ground. You do learn to play by yourself, but you are always aware that the other side is empty. Gradually, you get used to it, though—or at least resigned. And that's where I am, most of the time. Resigned.

I'm even getting resigned to that great yearning I once talked about, especially since it's nothing new. Looping back to the time before I met him, when I was young, I remember being consumed by yearning, though I never knew for what. I didn't feel it when we were together, but I feel it now. Could that yearning have been for him? Or could our being together have masked the earlier yearning? Just one of the many questions stirred up from the depths by grief.

Day 335, **Dear Jeff,**

I'm crying. Can barely see these words as I write. During the years of your dying, I could not face what you were going through, didn't even want to imagine my life without you. Well, now I don't have to imagine it—I am living it.

I am grateful that we reconnected at the end. It gave us a chance to apologize for any slights, to reaffirm our love, to remind us why we spent all those decades together.

One thing I always loved about you was that you were

such an appreciator. You appreciated the small things of life as well as the large. I still remember when you were in the emergency room waiting for your diagnosis, you were so grateful to be free of the pain, so appreciative of the warm blanket, so considerate of the doctor who gave you the bad news.

I have this idea in the back of my head that you died to set me free, but I didn't want to be free of you—only of your dying. It was incredibly painful watching you waste away to nothing. I wish I could have been present at your cremation. I was with you every step of the way except for that last one. Well, the second to last one. The last step won't be until I die, too.

I wish I could go back and tell you how much I loved you. I did tell you, but even I didn't know how much I loved you until you were gone from my life. You gave me so much—a safe place where I could let my mind roam knowing you were there to keep me centered. You were there. That's the key. I loved that you were there, always available to talk to, to prepare meals with, to do errands and chores with, to share the trivialities of the day. I once lamented that our great love had descended into trivialities, but now I see that sharing the trivialities of day-to-day life is what made our love great. Love isn't what you feel but what you do. And we did so much together. I don't mind doing things alone. I don't even mind being alone—I just can't bear your being gone from the face of the earth.

I still get that stepping-off-the-curb-into-nothingness feeling when I think of your being gone. So many tears, Jeff. The world is a much harsher place now that you are no longer here. I miss you more than I ever thought possible. For the rest of my life, I'll feel your absence.

Adios, compadre.

Day 338, Blog Post, **I Am an Eleven-Month Grief Survivor**

Eleven months ago, my life mate—my soul mate—died of inoperable kidney cancer. He took a final breath, his

Adam's apple bobbed twice, and then he was gone. It was a silent night—no storm lashing out in anger, no rain falling like tears, just the quiet passing of a quiet man. Nothing remained of him at the end but skin stretched around a skeleton without enough weight to make a dent in the bed, yet he left behind a hole in my life and my heart that will never be filled.

We'd been together thirty-four years. In comparison, eleven months seems like a mere blip in time, yet those few months contain an eon of sorrow and pain. He'd been dying for so long that I was glad when his suffering ended. Because of it, I truly did not expect to grieve, and I didn't at first. I just sat in the room with his body and waited for the funeral director. The people at the hospice care center wanted me to finish the night there, but I couldn't stay, so after they removed his body (not in a body bag but covered with a red plush blanket—he would have liked that), I headed back to the house. (You notice I don't say I headed back home? He was my home. The house was just a house.)

I'm not sure when the grief hit me, but when it did, it slammed into me with such force I have not yet recovered my balance. It wasn't a single body slam—the grief continued to grow for many weeks, until it all but consumed me. It didn't consume me, of course. I managed to do all the terrible tasks of death: the grim paperwork, the final bills, the disposition of his effects. I've even managed to get on with my life. I've made friends. I've gone to museums. I take care of myself most of the time. (I still don't always eat right, don't always exercise, though I do walk for miles almost every day.)

On meeting me, you'd never know of my sorrow. I laugh, talk, joke, act like a normal person. And I am normal. Grief is now part of my normalcy. Every Friday night and Saturday, it descends on me. (Though upsurges of grief can occur any time without warning.) I cannot go to sleep on Friday nights until after 1:40 am, the hour of his death. Even if I don't remember, my body does. And then, there is my time of the month—the date of his death. The 27th.

145

Yesterday I got an email from my sister: *Can I tell you something I just love about you? I love your sense of irony, your talent for observation of seemingly insignificant details, and your almost-spiritual gift for connecting dots across time and distance.* I thanked her, telling her I so needed to hear something nice, and she responded: *Well, considering it's Saturday, and considering the time of month, you just can't hear enough nice things today, that's what I'm thinking.*

My time of the month. That used to mean something completely different, but now it means only this: I survived another twenty-eight or thirty or thirty-one days without him.

Twelfth Month

Day 340, **Dear Jeff,**

So begins the countdown to the one-year anniversary of your death. I thought the day itself would be hard, but I've learned from this past month that the hardest days are those leading up to the anniversary.

My heart feels so broken, I react emotionally to everything. I'm hoping after the anniversary I'll be able to find my equilibrium. The further I get from you, the more lost I feel. Our life is gone, and I haven't yet found a new focus. I wish we were together, but we're not. I wish you hadn't been sick for so long, but you were. I wish you hadn't died, but you did. Those are the realities I have to face. I don't want to be one of those women who grieves so long grief becomes her life.

I wish I could see your smile once more. You didn't smile often that last year, but when you did, it lit up your face and lifted my spirits. I wish I could hear your gleeful laugh.

Take care of yourself. I'll take care of me so you don't have to worry.

Day 341, **Dear Jeff,**

Small things sometimes bring me comfort. Yesterday I closed my letter to you with the words, *"Take care of yourself. I'll take care of me so you don't have to worry."* Gave me comfort for some reason. Maybe because it made me feel we're still in this together? Have a combined focus but with a division of duties? We had a joint focus for decades, and sometimes it feels as if this is still "our" life but with all the chores of living now resting with me.

I should be grateful I had you for all those years, and I am, it's just . . . how can it be over? How can you be gone? That's the crux of my grief. Not that I'm missing you and yearning for you, but that you're dead. If you had left me for a better life, if you were happy and healthy, I'd miss you and would probably be furious with you, but I would take comfort in knowing that you're alive.

I worry about you (needlessly, since you aren't suffering. Even though it feels as if I'm reliving your last year, counting down the days to your death, you already died and cannot die again. All your suffering is behind you).

I try to be glad that you'll never have to suffer the infirmities of old age, but you already did. Your illness made you old. You looked and acted like you were in your eighties. About broke my heart. (Irritated me too, though why, I don't know. Did part of me think you were doing it on purpose? Oh, please no! I am not that terrible, am I?)

I'm going to have to let you go one of these days. You know that, don't you? I won't be abandoning you—I promise it's not that—but as I said yesterday, I don't want to be one of those women who mourns her dead mate the rest of her life. (Though I probably will.) Life is hard enough without carrying the weight of such sorrow. I'm not ready to let you go yet, Jeff. Your absence looms so large.

Day 343, **Grief Journal**

I still feel Jeff's absence from the earth, still miss him, still yearn for one more word or one more smile.

Today is Friday, and I'm crying again. Fridays and Saturdays are particularly hard for me. He died at 1:40 am on a Friday night (which made the actually date a Saturday) and my body can't decide which day is the right time to mourn, so my upsurge of grief spans both days. I say my body can't decide, because there is an element of physicality to grief, especially when it comes to the death of someone who shared more than three decades of your life. You feel his absence in your cells, in your marrow, in your blood. I can sometimes feel (or imagine I feel) his vibes still surrounding the things he used, the things we shared. I find myself stupidly hugging a dish before I use it, remembering him eating off that plate.

Most of our stuff is in storage because of my temporary

living arrangements. Yesterday, I felt a moment of panic when I realized that eventually I would unpack and begin using our household goods, that I would feel his energy permeating them. Usage will dissipate that energy, but for now, it's still there. Perhaps when I need those items, the psychic remnants of him will bring me comfort, the way using a few of our things bring me comfort now, but it could just as easily set off a whole new strata of pain.

But I won't—can't—think of that. It still takes almost everything I have just to get through the days, to concentrate on this day. I can live today. What is one day without him when we had so many? I am most at peace when I forget that he is dead, when somewhere in the far reaches of my mind I feel that he is back in the house we shared, waiting for me. It's not that I can't live without him. I can. It's that the world is such an alien place now that he is gone. I still remember how right the world felt when I met him. I had no expectations of having any more of him than that first relationship of customer (me) and storeowner (him), but back then, just knowing a person such as he existed made the world a more radiant place. When he died, he took the radiance with him.

I can't identify that specific quality of radiance he brought to my life. He was sick for so very long, we gradually untwinned our lives, he to dying, me to aloneness. And yet, that connection, that depth, that radiance remained until the end. In his last weeks we even found a renewed closeness, a renewed commitment, but before that, we endured months, maybe years of unhappiness.

And, childishly, I am still unhappy. I want what I cannot have. I try to find in myself the radiance (the center? the heart? the home?—whatever it was that he gave me). I will need that to keep me going through the coming decades, and I fear I am not enough. I feel empty. What if I truly am empty? At times, I think I have depths enough to plumb, other times those depths seem an illusion, an opaqueness that masks my shallows.

But what isn't shallow is how much I miss him. That

yearning is as deep as the Black Canyon.

Day 345, Blog Post, **The Ferris Wheel of Life**

Relationships, especially between long-term couples, change continuously, but we seldom notice those changes in the whirr and whirl of everyday life. Even our images of each other change to accommodate the passing years. We are always "us."

A day or two after my life mate died, I couldn't visualize him, so I looked at the only photo I have of us, and I wept because I did not recognize him. Fifteen years ago, when that photo was taken, it was an exact likeness of him, but during the years of illness, he lost the fullness in his face, first becoming distinguished looking, then gaunt. I have an idea/image of him in my mind, perhaps a composite of him through the years, perhaps what he actually looked like near the end, and that single photo I have of him does not resemble the person I knew. One more thing to mourn.

That is the problem with grief, there is always one more thing to mourn.

It's not just our internal images of a person that changes to accommodate the vagaries of age; our internal image of the relationship itself changes to accommodate the vagaries of life. Most of the transformation of a relationship from youthful and passionate to aged and (perhaps) wise and companionable goes unnoticed. We are always who we are. We are always in the present.

The big events of life—starting a business or losing one, having children or losing them—we celebrate or grieve as the case may be, but other things disappear without acknowledgement. We used to walk together, ride bikes, play tennis, kick a soccer ball, but such activities were supplanted with other, more sedentary activities as his health deteriorated. But still, there we were, on the great Ferris wheel of our relationship—always current, always us. And then he died.

When one of a couple dies, the Ferris wheel of your shared life comes to a halt. Those who have not experienced the loss of a long-time mate think that the Ferris wheel continues with the survivor, but that isn't true. It looms there, empty. The continually evolving, revolving living relationship is dead. All you have is what has already happened, and now you can see every transformation throughout all the years. You don't simply mourn the man he was at the end, you also mourn the man you met and the various men he became during the subsequent years. And you grieve for all those little things that passed unnoticed during the course of your relationship. They didn't matter while you were together because you were together, but now they add to the overwhelming whole of grief.

Gradually, the survivor climbs aboard another Ferris wheel of her own, but the original one still haunts. If I live long enough, my grief will fade and perhaps disappear in the whirr and whirl of everyday life, but for now, newly recalled memories keep seeping into my life, and they have to be processed, mourned, dealt with. Sometimes these are minor issues, sometimes major. And all a surprise. How could so much have happened during those quiet years?

One recurring theme in our lives was vitamins and other food supplements. We met at his health food store. The first time we connected physically was when he handed me a bottle of vitamin A and our touch lingered. The first time our gazes locked was over his checkout counter. The supplement regimen he created for me changed as new research came out, but always, there were the supplements, a symbol of how much he cared for me. Now all that loss has to be dealt with somehow.

And that is just one aspect of our shared life. There were almost 34 years worth of good things and bad. 408 months. 1756 weeks. 12,296 days. When he was alive, all those days blended together, but now each exists separately, a thing in itself. A thing to be mourned. No wonder grief is such a major undertaking.

Day 347, Grief Journal

After Jeff died, I told myself, "If you can just get through the first month, you'll be fine." I wasn't. So then I told myself, "After the third month, you'll be fine." The months passed, and I still grieved, so I told myself, "After six months . . ." And, "after a year." I'm nearing that first anniversary, but I don't seem to be completely shedding my grief. Grief follows its own time. It will not, cannot be rushed. Even worse, I seem to be keyed into this same month last year—the final month of his life—and I feel as if I'm counting down to his death . . . again. The big difference is that last year I did not give in to emotion—at least not much and not until the end. His care was all that mattered. Well, I'm feeling now what I didn't feel then. And just like last year, nothing I do can make him well.

If that's not enough trauma for one month, this will be my first birthday without him, and oddly, it saddens me. We didn't celebrate our birthdays. Sometimes we acknowledged them, sometimes we didn't, but they were no big deal, just a change of numbers, so I've been wondering why this birthday troubles me, and tonight I figured it out. This is one of one of the big 0 birthdays, the one where you can no longer fool yourself into thinking you are still young. (Even the actuarial tables acknowledge this one as a major change). And here's the kicker: Jeff and I will not be growing old together. There will be no walking hand-in-hand in our twilight years, no reminiscing about our youth, no helping each other overcome the infirmities of age. "The end" has been written on our love story.

So, here I am, at the beginning of this auspicious month, standing tearfully on the cusp of . . . what? I don't know.

Day 352, Blog Post, **Going Along for the Ride**

Life takes odd twists and turns. It seemed to me, when my life-mate—my soul mate—was dying of inoperable kidney cancer, that our lives would never change. He'd been sick for so long, dying cell by cell, that it felt as if we were locked in a horror show of endless, predictable misery. Last year at this time, his disintegration suddenly speeded up, and he started dying organ by organ. And then he was gone.

152

I've made no secret of my grief, of the pain his "goneness" has caused me, but through it all, I've been getting on with my life, trying to open myself to new experiences, trying to hope for . . . what? That is the kicker. How do you know what to hope for if you can't even imagine where you are headed?

A couple days ago I sat in a restaurant, one thousand miles from our home, celebrating my birthday with new friends and acquaintances I'd met through a grief support group. Though all nine of us are trying to deal with the devastating loss of a loved one, we talked and laughed and had a good time. It showed me that there is life after death—we lived despite our loved ones' deaths. And it showed me something else. That for all of life's seeming predictability, it can still surprise. A year ago, when my life mate was a couple of weeks from death, there is no way I could ever have envisioned that restaurant scene.

Back then, I knew I'd have to leave our home, to find a temporary haven where I could deal with my grief, but I had no clear idea of where I wanted to go, and somehow I found myself in the desert. And, since I'd been a virtual hermit for years, I could never have guessed that I would make so many friends. Nor had I celebrated my birthday in . . . well, never mind how many years it's been. And yet, there I was, with new friends in a time and place I couldn't have even imagined a year ago.

So where am I going? How will I get there? Who will I be? Who will I be with? There is no way of knowing. I'll just have to go along for the ride and hope that everything works out when I get there. Wherever "there" is.

Day 358, **Dear Jeff**

It's Saturday again. Last night I couldn't sleep until after my "witching" hour—the hour of your death. Sometimes it seems as if I'm always leading into Saturday or dealing with it. I am so tired of being sad. Even if I keep busy, grief surges at times. It's a very physical thing. I can sometimes keep from feeling it emotionally or mentally, but then I can feel it in my bones, in my very cells.

I once heard that every seven years a person's cells completely turn over, so that in seven years you become a different person. In seven years, then, maybe I won't feel such yearning for you since you won't be written into the fabric of new cells. And we will no longer be sharing viruses that carry cell information from one to the other of us.

It seems unreal that it's been almost a year since I've seen you, even more unreal that I'm still grieving. I don't think about you all the time. Sometimes I can barely remember what you looked like, barely remember that we once shared a life, but the sadness, the cell-deep sadness is always with me. I miss you with all my being.

Sometimes when I get frustrated with not being able to see you or understand your goneness, I beat the air to relieve some of the tension. I just piston my arms. Want to hear something funny? You know how in movies when a martial artist kicks or punches, it's accompanied by a whoosh like birds' wings? I always thought that was phony, but occasionally when I am venting my frustration on the poor defenseless air, I hear that sound.

I try not to think of the bleak future stretching before me because it might not be bleak. No matter what happens, though, you'll still be dead. My being happy doesn't change that, doesn't make up for it.

I've been wondering if my task during this time is to continue differentiating myself from you, but if that's the point of all this, then why were we ever together? There are too many contradictory thoughts battling it out in my head. When life makes sense, death doesn't. When death makes sense, life doesn't. When togetherness makes sense, aloneness doesn't. When aloneness makes sense, togetherness doesn't. Such thoughts are probably a waste of brainpower, but with you gone, this is all I'm left with—a mind circling endlessly upon itself with no one to stop the whirl.

Take care of yourself, Jeff, and I'll take care of me. That's what it's about, isn't it? Taking care of ourselves and each other until time runs out. Adios, compadre.

Day 359, **Dear Jeff,**

I never felt as if I were wasting time no matter what you and I did—even something trivial like playing a game or watching a movie—so why do I feel I'm wasting time if I do those things alone? Don't I have just as much worth now that I'm alone as I did when I was with you?

When I was out walking in the desert yesterday, I talked to you. You didn't answer, of course, or if you did, I didn't hear. We talked about meaninglessness. If you still exist somewhere, if you still have being, if life doesn't end with death, then life has an inherent meaning—whatever I do or think or feel, no matter how trivial, has meaning because it adds to the Eternal Everything. If death brings nothing but oblivion, then there is no intrinsic meaning to life. So a search for meaning is meaningless (except on a practical level. We all need to feel we are doing something meaningful so we can get through our days and even thrive). Life either has meaning or it doesn't. Meaning isn't something to find but to be. So, I'm going to search for meaninglessness, or at least accept it.

Such thoughts seem as meaningless and as trivial as the rest of life. They get me knowhere. (I'm leaving that error, because . . . wow! So perfect!)

I've been watching your Boston Legal tapes again. Nicely meaningless since they put me to sleep. But they make me feel connected to you because we watched them a year ago during your last days at home.

This first year of your being dead is coming to an end, and I still don't know how to survive the pain of your being gone, but I am surviving. Not thriving, not yet, but I will. There's still so much to work through—all those years of your being ill, our unhappiness, our shattered dreams. Despite all the bad, we did have a good life, a fulfilling one. We journeyed together as long as we could, now it's up to me to continue our journey alone. Will it continue to be "our" journey or will it become mine alone? I know who I was when I was with you. Now I need to find out who I am without you. To find worth in being alone.

Adios, compadre. I love you.

Day 361. Blog Post, **Grief and Remembrance**

The problem with grief is that while the subject of the grief stays gone, grief comes again and again, sometimes when one is least expecting it. I'd been doing well handling my grief after the death of the man with whom I spent thirty-four years of my life, yet these past couple of days grief has come to revisit me, and my sorrow is as great as it was a year ago.

I mentioned before about the terrible anniversaries of my grief. I lived through the first anniversary of the day pain struck him with such force that he took to bed for the rest of his life. I lived through the first anniversary of the day we got the diagnosis: inoperable kidney cancer. I lived through the first anniversary of the day we signed up for hospice, of the day we signed the DNR (the do not resuscitate order).

I had a hiatus of a couple of weeks where I was mostly at peace, then yesterday I was so overcome with grief that I wanted to scream out in anguish. I couldn't figure out what hit me or why, but as it happens, the body remembers even when the mind doesn't, and my body remembered that yesterday was the first anniversary of the last time we hugged, the last time we kissed.

And today . . . today is the first anniversary of the last time we talked. The last time he spoke to me. The last time he knew who I was. Today is also the anniversary of the day we took him to the hospice care center to live out the remaining few days of his life.

I'd been looking forward to the anniversary of his death, supposing that after a year of grieving I would be mostly finished with the pain, that he would have receded from my thoughts. It was a realistic expectation—my focus on him has been diminishing, so much so that sometimes it feels as if our life together was a story I told myself long ago—but as always, grief has its own agenda.

The past year seems to have disappeared. I know I lived it, know what I accomplished (and what I didn't) yet the cliché is true—it passed in the blink of an eye. If I turn my head quickly, perhaps I will see him. He feels that close. If the world could turn back for just a second, I could catch him. Hang on to him. Never let him go.

But he is gone. And all the tears I shed this year will never bring him back.

Today was my grief support group day. I'd stopped going for a while because I wasn't in the same place as the other bereft, and I was afraid I was doing them a disservice by my dissociation. After a few weeks, I went back to be there for a friend, and today she and the group were there for me. Since I hadn't had a memorial service for my mate, the facilitator asked me to say a eulogy, to make sense of his life, but I couldn't make sense of it—I don't understand the point of his having had to suffer so much. I could make sense of his life as pertains to me, though. I talked about how he accompanied and mentored me on my journey—my quest for truth and meaning—how he went with me as far as he could. We'd used up our relationship, not in a bad way, but in a good way. We'd talked for hours on end, day after day, year after year. We read books and discussed them, studied films, researched various topics and shared information, tried to see the big picture and connect all the disparate parts of life.

I want so much to talk with him once more, to have one of those electric conversations where ideas were zinging back and forth, but the truth is, we said everything that was important. I have not come up with a single question for him this past year that he had not already answered. (Except for what he wants done with his ashes, but even that is an answer. If he cared, he would have told me.)

The last thing he ever said to me was, "Remember everything I told you."

And I do remember.

Day 363 Blog Post, **Grief: Counting Down to the First Anniversary**

In three days it will be a year since the death of my life mate—my soul mate. I've been counting down the days with tears. I would have thought I'd have finished my weeping months ago, and for the most part I have, but here it comes again. I've been keeping busy, not wanting to drown in sorrow. In fact, I'll be leaving in a few minutes to have lunch with friends. Like me, they lost their mates, and so their presence is a comfort. We'll laugh and talk, and that will keep the tears at bay, but when I get back to the house, I'll probably be sad again. And that's okay. I'm finding that now, after a wave of intense grief, there is a backwash of peace.

The anniversary itself was supposed to have been a good day for me, not a celebration so much as an acknowledgement that I survived the year. And perhaps it will be a good day despite the upsurge in sorrow. My latest book, *Light Bringer*—the last one he helped me research and edit, the last one I read to him as I was writing it—will be published on his death day as a memorial to him. The book is his epitaph, his tombstone, the final resting place for our joint efforts. (There is one more book he influenced, but that book is only half finished, and I haven't had the heart to work on it.)

During all this year, I haven't been able to eat the foods we fixed together (with the exception of salads. Those I still can eat, though why, I don't know since salads were a major component of our meals). So I thought a good sign of my healing would be to fix one of those meals I haven't been able to eat. Today I am going to get the ingredients for his chili, and on the anniversary, I will cook a batch in his honor. I will probably watch a movie that he taped for us, which is what we always did on special occasions.

He would have enjoyed such a day. I wish with everything I have that he were here, but of course, if he were here, there would be no such anniversary to endure, to acknowledge, yes, even to celebrate.

Day 364, Blog Post, **Keeping Vigil**

I'm continuing my anniversary vigil, reliving the days that led up to the death of my life mate, my soul mate. This vigil is not so much conscious as subconscious, a feeling that the events of a year ago are happening again. Part of me seems to think I really am there at his deathbed—when I was out walking in the desert today, I found myself wailing, "Don't go! Please don't leave me!"

This is so different from last year's reality. Then, I was concentrating on him, on his suffering, on his need to let go of life, and I never once thought of asking him to stay for me. Would never have subjected him to more pain and suffering. Would never have wished him more days as a helpless invalid. And yet, here I am, today, begging him not to leave me.

Such is grief—a place where time goes backward and forward, stands still and zips ahead.

Perhaps when this first terrible year is finished, when I have experienced this reprise of his death from my point of view rather than his, I will be able to put a lot of my grief behind me and go forward with my life. Though I still don't know what that life is, where it will take me, or if it will take me anywhere at all. Perhaps all that is necessary is to experience life, and if that is true, well, I have certainly lived this past year.

It's strange looking back to the long years of his dying. I thought I was ready to leave the emotional burdens and the financial constraints of his illness behind. I thought I was ready to live out my life alone. I even looked forward to the challenges, especially since he told me that when he was gone, things would come together for me. He was a bit of a seer (though he mostly saw doom) so I believed him. But neither of us expected the toll grief would take. (Well, he might have suspected. He was very concerned about me.) I knew I'd be okay, and I am, but I didn't understand what grief was. (I'd already lost a brother and my mother, but that was not the same as losing my cosmic twin, the person who shared my thoughts and dreams, who lived in the same world I did.) I never expected the sheer physicality of grief, the physical wrenching, the feeling of amputation, the feeling of psychic starvation, the feeling of imbalance in the world, the sheer goneness of him.

Nor did I expect to still be worrying about him. Is he okay? Is his suffering really over?

His death was not a silent one. He moaned for days, though the nurses assured me he was feeling no pain, that he was sighing, that it was a common reaction for those who were dying. I remember standing there, exactly one year ago tonight, listening to him, worrying that he was suffering, and then one of his "sighs" became lyrical, almost like a note from a song, and I knew he was telling me he was all right.

I keep listening for some sound, looking for some sign that he is okay, but today all I hear is silence.

Day 365, **Grief Journal,**

Tomorrow is the anniversary of Jeff's death. I've never had a year go by so fast—at least in retrospect. The days themselves were long and agonizing. One year doesn't seem like much in comparison to the decades we shared, but it's one year further from our life together and one year closer to my death.

Shouldn't I have learned something from this experience? Shouldn't I have become wiser? More mature? Marked somehow by death's shadow? I've always wanted to be other than I am—better, stronger, radiant—so perhaps this is the lesson of grief: I am who I am, for better or for worse.

This is an even harder lesson: You can get through grief. You can learn to live without him. You can find happiness again by living one day at a time. But the dead are still dead, and nothing you do can ever change that.

That is what drives my grief. Not the self-pity that sometimes breaks through my wall of courage, not the sustained note of sadness that keens beneath my consciousness, but the awareness that he is gone. He no longer cares that he suffered for years with an ailment the doctors couldn't diagnose until it was too late. He no longer cares that he will never again watch any of his favorite movies or read a book. He no longer cares that he will never go on another road trip. He no longer cares that he will never again walk or talk or eat or smile.

But I care.

Perhaps it is foolish of me still to care for and about someone who is beyond caring, but I cared immensely for him while he was alive, so why would I stop now that he is dead? He may no longer have feelings, but I do. Once he was alive and now he is not. Why shouldn't I care about that?

There is an element of self-pity when it comes to grief, but self-pity is not all there is. Grief is a vast network of emotional, spiritual, and physical reactions, and part of that is sorrow on behalf of the one who died.

If grief is just about me (and perhaps someday I'll get to the point where it is only about me), then it's not my place to care that he is gone from this earth. But if life is worth living, how can I not care that it is being denied him?

The corollary is, if he is the one who got the better end of the deal, if he truly is in a better place, then why am I still here? But I'd just as soon not dwell on that.

Day 366, Blog Post, **I Am a Twelve-Month Grief Survivor**
Twelve months.

One full year.

It seems impossible that my life mate—my soul mate—has been gone for so long. It seems even more impossible that I've survived.

His death came as no surprise. I'd seen all the end signs: his unending restlessness, his inability to swallow, his disorientation, his wasting away to nothing, the change in his breathing. Nor did my reaction come as a surprise. I was relieved he'd finally been able to let go and that his suffering (and the indignities of dying) had stopped. I was relieved his worst fear (lingering or a long time as a helpless invalid) had not had a chance to materialize. What did come as a surprise was my grief. I'd had years to come to terms with his dying. I'd gone through all the stages of grief, so I thought the only thing left was to get on with my life. And yet . . . there it was. His death seemed to have created a rupture in the very fabric of my being—a soulquake. The world felt skewed with him gone, and I had a hard time gaining my balance. Even now, I sometimes experience a moment of panic, as if I am setting a foot onto empty space when I expected solid ground.

I have no idea how I survived the first month, the second, the twelfth. All I know is that I did survive. I'm even healing. I used to think "healing" was an odd word to use in conjunction with grief since grief is not an illness, but I have learned that what needs to heal is that rupture—one cannot continue to live for very long with a bloody psyche. The rupture caused by his dying doesn't yawn as wide as it once did, and the raw edges are finally scarring over. I don't steel myself against the pain of living as I had been. I'm even looking forward, curious to see what the future holds in store for me.

I am not ashamed of all the tears I've shed this past year, nor am I ashamed of making it known how much I've mourned. The tears themselves are simply a way of easing the terrible stress of grief, a way of releasing chemicals that built because of the stress. And by making my grief public, I've met so many wonderful people who are also undertaking this journey.

I've been saying all along that I'll be okay eventually, but the truth is, despite my ever-present sorrow, my yearning for him, and the agonizing upsurges in grief, I am doing okay now. I will always grieve for him, always miss him, maybe always cry for him, but I will survive.

I expected this to be a day of sadness, but it is one of gladness. I am glad he shared his life (and his death) with me. Glad we had so many years together. Glad we managed to say everything that was necessary while we still had time. Tomorrow will be soon enough to try to figure out what I am going to do now that my first year of mourning is behind me. Today I am going to watch one of his favorite movies, eat a bowl of his chili (his because he created the recipe, his because he was the one who always fixed it), and celebrate his life.

Afterward

Everything that happened since the death of my life mate—my soul mate—has surprised me. No, not surprised me. Shocked me.

I was shocked that the end came so quickly. He'd been sick such a very long time, his health fading slowly, that his dying became our way of life. When he was finally diagnosed with inoperable kidney cancer, we were told he had three to six months to live. He had only three weeks. And those weeks seemed to evaporate in just a few hours.

After he died, I was shocked by the very presence of grief. My brother died four and a half years ago, and my mother died a year later. I handled both deaths well, so I thought I could cope with the death of my mate. I didn't know, had no way of knowing, that one didn't grieve the same for every loss. I didn't know, had no way of knowing, that the death of a long time mate would feel like an amputation.

After he died, I was shocked by the depth and breadth of my feelings. During the last year of his life, and especially the last six months, he'd begun withdrawing from the world and from me. This withdrawal, this lessening of a need to be with others is a natural part of dying, and my response to his withdrawal was just as natural—an increased determination to live. He might have been dying but I wasn't, and I had to untangle our lives, find a way to survive his dying and his death. I thought I had successfully completed this task, but his death rocked me to the core of my being.

After he died, I was shocked by his sheer goneness. Because I'd spent so much time alone that last year, I thought life without him would feel much the same, but it isn't like he is in another room or another city or another country— it's like nothing I'd ever experienced before. I still have no words to describe the finality, the undoableness, the vacuum of death. He was part of my life for thirty-four years. We breathed the same air. We were connected by our thoughts, our shared experiences, the zillion words we'd spoken to each other. And then he was gone from this earth. Erased. Deleted. I still can't wrap my mind around that.

After he died, I was shocked that I felt so shattered. So broken. And I am shocked that I still feel that way at times. I am shocked that no matter how strong you are, how well you are healing, grief can slam into you at any time, especially after a good day when you're not expecting it, and the pain feels as raw as it was at the beginning.

After he died, I was shocked by the scope of grief. You grieve for the one who died and you grieve for yourself because you have to live without him. You grieve for all the things you did and the things you didn't do. You grieve for what went wrong in your shared life and what went right. You grieve for the past and you grieve for the lost future. You grieve for all the hopes and dreams and possibilities that died with him. It's amazing that anyone can survive all that pain, but we do, and that shocks me, too.

After he died, I was shocked by how physical grief is. You experience changes in brain chemistry, in hormones, in equilibrium. Injuries and illnesses heal much more slowly than normal. Higher levels of adrenaline keep you from sleeping. Stress depletes what little reserves you have. You have trouble concentrating, trouble gripping (you drop things more frequently). You experience dizziness and nausea. Your skin thirsts for his touch. And you have a higher death rate from all causes than non-grievers.

After he died, I was shocked by how complicated human emotions can be. You can feel sad and unsad at the same time. You can be determined to live, yet not care if you live or die. You can know in your depths he's gone, but still listen for him, still long for him, still worry about him.

After he died, I was shocked that I am still the same person I was before he died. Such trauma should have changed me, made me stronger and wiser perhaps, yet I'm still just me. Sadder, but still recognizably me.

Most of all, I'm shocked to discover that life really does

go on. As this book goes to press, my second year of grief is ending. I've learned not to get too hungry, angry, lonely, or tired, since any of those states can bring an upsurge of grief. Although I'm willing to let grief take its course, I have no desire to let it rule the rest of my life. I intend to be bold and adventurous, to embrace new possibilities, to renew my spontaneity, enthusiasm and independence. But before that can happen, I need to stretch a bit more, need to grow.

From the beginning (odd how I always refer to my onset of grief as the "beginning," when that time seemed to be all about "endings"), I tried to break grief down into its various components to demystify it and make it more manageable. When grief is new, one is bombarded with so many emotions, physical responses, and mental gymnastics that it is almost impossible to see/know/feel what is happening. As time passes and the bombardment slows, it becomes easier to separate the feelings into categories and deal with them. As time continues to pass, some of the components of grief dissipate (such as the panic, the need to scream, the confusion) and some disappear (such as the nausea, dizziness, difficulty breathing, inability to eat or inability to stop eating). But the knowledge that the world is forever altered because your loved one is dead still remains.

I miss Jeff and yearn desperately for one more word from him, one more smile, but I can deal with that now—I've mostly grown used to the yearning. I can also remember him and our shared life without breaking down. I can deal with what life throws at me even though he is no longer by my side. And I'm learning to deal with the loneliness and the aloneness. But what I can't deal with is his being dead.

He is gone, and there is nothing I can do about it. I keep re-realizing those two simple facts. I do not think our brains are wired to understand the sheer goneness of death. A lot of grief has to do with the mind disconnect that happens when you realize your loved one is no longer here on earth. It's as if for a second you open up to a cosmic reality or an eternal truth. The façade of life shatters, and through the cracks you can almost see, almost sense, almost know . . .

That is where my mind hits a wall and causes so much pain I start crying.

I now know those grief bursts are growing pains. My mind/spirit/psyche is trying to stretch so it can understand why he is not here, why I can't see him or hear him, why he is so very gone. Maybe my grief will burn itself out before my mind stretches enough to encompass such an enormous thought, but maybe, just maybe, I'll get to where I need to be.

Acknowledgments

I would like to thank everyone who offered support and encouragement during the first terrible year of my grief. Your words and hugs, both virtual and real, helped more than you will ever know.

In particular, I'd like to thank:

The Reverend Dr. Michael David Simpson for his practical suggestions, such as keeping Jeff's ashes, which brought me tremendous comfort;

Joylene Butler, Carol Garvin, and my blog readers for their heartbreaking and heartwarming comments;

Pat Shaw, John Philipp, and the Writin' Wombats for offering solace and encouragement;

Deanna Dolf, Tim Smith and the rest of my grief group for their support.

Leesa Healy, Annie Brier, Malcolm Campbell, and Brenda Wallace, who read the manuscript and offered valuable insights.

I'd especially like to thank Jan D. Linton, my sister in sorrow. She lost her mate four months after I lost Jeff, and though she lives on the opposite side of the country, she has been my companion on this terrible quest. I wish with all my heart neither of us ever had to embark on this journey, but I'm honored she shared her grief with me.

To readers of *Grief: The Great Yearning*: thank you for reading my story. If you would like to send me a message, tell me about your grief, or ask a question, you can leave a comment on my blog: www.ptbertram.wordpress.com or contact me through my website: www.patbertram.com.

Other Titles available from Pat Bertram and Indigo Sea Press.

A Spark of Heavenly Fire
Pat Bertram
In quarantined Colorado, where hundreds of thousands of people are dying from an unstoppable, bio-engineered disease, investigative reporter Greg Pullman risks everything to discover the truth: Who unleashed the deadly organism? And why?

More Deaths Than One
Pat Bertram
Bob Stark returns to Denver after 18 years in SE Asia to discover that the mother he buried before he left is dead again. At her new funeral, he sees . . . himself. Is his other self a hoaxer? A doppelganger? Or is something more sinister going on?

Daughter Am I
Pat Bertram
When twenty-five-year-old Mary Stuart inherits a farm from her recently murdered grandparents -- grand-parents her father claimed had died before she was born -- she becomes obsessed with finding out who they were and why someone wanted them dead.

Light Bringer
Pat Bertram

Thirty-seven years after being abandoned on the doorstep of a remote cabin in Colorado, Becka Johnson returns to try to discover her identity, but she only finds more questions. Who has been looking for her all those years? And why?

Excerpt from *Light Bringer*

Philip spied a woman about his own age in the parking lot of the rustic shopping center and hobbled outside.

She looked just as he remembered. The lithe body that moved as gracefully and effortlessly as a song wafting on a breeze. The shoulder-length brown hair that glimmered red and gold in the sunlight. The smile, big and bright and welcoming. Only her clothes—a pale green blouse and cotton shorts—struck a discordant note, as if he were used to seeing her in more exotic attire.

"Hello," she said when he neared. The single word sounded as musical as an entire symphony.

"Hello," he said, a goofy grin stretching his face. He felt a harmonic resonance and knew, once again, they belonged together.

After several seconds, her smile faded. "Do I know you?"

"Of course. We met . . ."

He gazed at her. Where had they met? Though it seemed as if he had always known her, they must have met somewhere, sometime; but when, in his pathetic little life, could he have met anyone so special? It slowly dawned on him he couldn't have—not until this very moment.

Ducking his head, he whispered, "I've made a terrible mistake. We don't know . . . We've never . . ."

Made in the USA
Monee, IL
18 May 2020